"power 10"
LEADERSHIP

HOW TO ENGAGE PEOPLE AND GET RESULTS

Dedicated to
those in management positions
who are committed to being
the best leaders they can be.

Printed by CreateSpace
ISBN: 1453790691
EAN-13: 9781453790694
Library of Congress Catalog Card Number: 2011900746

This publication is designed to provide accurate and authoritative information in regard to the subject matter covered. It is sold with the understanding that the printer is not engaged in rendering legal, accounting, or other professional services. If legal advice or other expert assistance is required, the services of a competent professional person should be sought.

For information about special discounts for bulk purchases, contact us through www.businesspaths.net

Printed in the United States of America

"power 10" LEADERSHIP

HOW TO ENGAGE PEOPLE AND GET RESULTS

Linda Oien

"power10" LEADERSHIP

Contents

Acknowledgments

I am truly grateful to a wide variety of people who, over the years, have helped make this book possible. Many contributed to my passion for leadership as I worked with and for them. Others provided insights and inspiration that shaped my philosophy and approach. Many offered encouragement from inception through publication of the book.

Since entering the leadership ranks, I've believed that training and development needs to reach beyond concept and theory and bring practical application to life. This, coupled with a decline in organizational commitment to professional development, has placed the success of many people in management positions at risk. As a result, organizations struggle to pull ahead of the competition and win the race.

That is why I've written this book…to help those in management and leadership positions function effectively in their role, engage people in running the business, and deliver consistent results.

So, thank you to the experts who have led the way for many of us:
Warren Bennis, Ken Blanchard, Steven Covey, John Kotter, John Maxwell, Phillip Oncken.

To the best leader I had the pleasure to work for, Steven Ramirez . He has the best balance between people and business I've ever experienced.

To the many people who worked with and for me over the years, who reinforced the fact that the people doing the work every day are the organization's most valuable asset. When you bring them all together, focused on a common goal, there is nothing they can't accomplish…magic happens!

To my consulting colleagues who vigorously discussed and debated a wide variety of topics over the years, Denny Beier, Reed Daugherity, and Jerry Haupt.

The many clients I have had the honor to work with and learn from over the years.

Deb Brady and Cher Merrill who read my manuscript, as it was being developed and provided writing, content, and format insights and recommendations.

Melissa Flint and Courtney Hasse, Head Women's Rowing Coach and Assistant Women's Rowing Coach at Gonzaga University, who so graciously opened a door into the world of rowing and the role of the Coxswain.

The alumni of the Gonzaga University Women's Rowing Team who agreed to have their photos included in "power10" Leadership.

Steve Malmquist, a high school friend who re-entered my life after twenty plus years at the precise moment I needed his expertise to get my manuscript ready for electronic submission to the editor and designers.

And last, but certainly not least, to my dear friends and family who believe in me, who have encouraged me to write and share my expertise and to keep moving forward with the book even when it seemed nearly hopeless.

Gonzaga University

Women's Rowing Team

Lauren Miller, Alissa Stempson

Alissa Stempson, Liz Moore

Sophie Bluhm, Lana Bowie, Lauren Miller

Liz Moore, Alissa Stempson

Spokane River

Preface

Introducing "power10" Leadership

It is said that rowers are probably the world's best athletes. The sport requires a full-body workout from members of the crew. Though rowing looks graceful, elegant, and sometimes effortless, it takes hard work, coordination, and precision to end up on the medal stand. The Coxswain (pronounced käk-sən), steers the boat, keeping it on the most direct course to ensure the fastest speed and accuracy. Perhaps more importantly, he or she motivates the rowers, coordinates the actions, and serves as their on-the-water coach. As such, the Coxswain will often call for the rowers to do a *"power10"*...ten of their best, perfectly timed, most powerful strokes...a strategy used to pull ahead of a competitor in the race.

In the same way, you as a leader have similar responsibility to the Coxswain in rowing—you're the on-the-floor coach in charge of directing, motivating, and coordinating your crew as they deliver performance and cross the finish line. Through your leadership, coaching, and your call for an occasional *"power10,"* you will ensure that your team or organization does its best, stays the course, and delivers results, because they are all making every stroke count.

That is why I've written this book...to help those in management and leadership positions function effectively in their role, engage people in running the business, and deliver consistent and sustainable results.

"power10" Leadership offers ten powerful chapters—the *"power10" success factors*—that will assist you in moving your crew into the lead, position it ahead of the competition, and win the race.

Get everyone in the boat rowing the same direction

The Coxswain makes sure that everyone is in the boat in preparation for the race. They ensure that the crew understands and is truly engaged in achieving the same goal—to be the first to cross the finish line. Without question in rowing, crossing the finish line can only happen if all crewmembers are rowing in the same direction.

For organizations, the same is true. To succeed as a winning organization requires that everyone in a management position fully understands his/her leadership role and sets the direction and tone for his or her people. Managers' ability to motivate, coach, and develop their people, coupled with knowing when to call for a *"power10,"* ensures that their team delivers the needed results and contributes to the achievement of organizational goals.

Let me share a *"power10"* example with you: I remember taking over a team that was working very hard, but they were not working smart. People were on the verge of burnout. Deadlines were missed, rework choked output, customers were unhappy, and people found it hard to get up and come to work every day. It was clear that we had to ensure that things were done right the first time, because there wasn't time to do them again.

Though it may have seemed like there was no way we could take time to step back and re-group, I knew the downward spiral would continue if not addressed. So we took a step back, examined key work processes, added strategically-placed quality checks, and clarified each person's role in the process. In other words, we got everyone rowing in the same direction.

As in the world of rowing, teamwork is number one, and good crews are made up of people willing to sacrifice their personal goals for the success of the team. So, everyone committed to functioning in his or her roles and following the updated processes.

Progress made during the first couple of weeks gave people hope that they really could get on top of the workload. With a *"power10" Leadership* approach and renewed team focus, it didn't take long to start seeing the results. Within the next month, the team actually caught up, and overtime was no longer needed!

The team felt confident in its ability to minimize errors and keep up with the ongoing demand. With regular focus and continuous improvements, within a year, the team was recognized as the most profitable in the district and it went on to become the national benchmark for productivity and cost effectiveness. This approach could be useful to you as a leader.

As you chart and navigate your course into the future, it is critical to develop leadership at all levels of the organization. As leader of your team, your role is similar to that of the Coxswain. You are the one who sets the pace and tone and motivates everyone in the boat to row toward the finish line. The effectiveness of your leadership will play a vital role in dealing with the changing currents and many challenges that lie ahead.

"power10" Leadership is designed to show you how to be your organization's Coxswain—a leader who can take your team to the medal stand every time. This book provides valuable insights, practical tools, and sound advice to help you get everyone in the boat rowing the same direction. You will be able to assess current performance against ten *"power10"* success factors, prioritize areas that need focus, and take action. *"power10" Leadership* will also help you affect change and increase commitment at all levels of the organization. Moreover, when customer and business situations warrant, you will know how to call for a *"power10"* to usher your boat and crew successfully across

the finish line. When you apply the principles and actions described in *"power10" Leadership*, your team and organization will be more effective, ready to compete in the race, and posed to cross the finish line first.

Call for a "power10" from your team or organization!

How to use this book

How to get the most from "power10" Leadership

If you find that keeping pace with todays changing environment poses many challenges for you, you are certainly not alone. Just finding the time to address areas that you know will have a long-term impact can be a real challenge.

During my earliest years in leadership, much of the training I received was based in concept and theory. As a consequence, I had to figure out ways on my own to help members of my team practically apply what they had learned. It was very time consuming, but I believed it was critically important. Theories are great, but with the challenges leaders face, they are looking for practical solutions.

"power10" Leadership recognizes that not every team, department, or organization is the same. They have different strengths, face unique challenges, and have a variety of approaches to their business. So, as the leader, the quicker you know where to start and isolate the priorities, the sooner you can engage people and get results.

This is a true "work" book:

"power10" Leadership is not the kind of book you sit down and read from cover to cover. It is designed with the busy manager and leader in mind. It is a book you will want to keep handy—not gathering dust on a bookshelf. It will serve as a valuable resource in your continuous improvement efforts.

You can use only those chapters that address your unique needs because it helps you:

- Pinpoint two to three *"power10"* success factors that need the most work
- Go to those respective chapters
- Take a closer look at what is contributing to the assessment, and
- Develop and implement actions to positively impact team or organizational effectiveness
- Enjoy the increased effectiveness and results

As you can see, you will use only a few chapters to begin getting everyone in the boat rowing the same direction!

"power10" Leadership is a book that can help you lead your team or organization through the many challenges you face in today's and tomorrow's business environment.

I sincerely hope that *"power10" Leadership* will make your job easier, save you time, and help you become more effective in your leadership role.

Let *"power10" success factors guide you!*

"power10" Leadership includes ten *"power10" success factors* for organizations and teams, ranging from communication to team development to getting results. The more areas a team or organization does well in, the more apt they are to pull ahead of the competition, cross the finish line, and end up on the medal stand. Front-line managers and executives alike find these *"power10"* success factors both relevant and useful.

1. Prepare for your "power10" Leadership journey

As you begin your *"power10" Leadership* journey, I highly recommend reading the chapter entitled "On Managing and Leading," followed with the chapter on "Your Leadership Role." These chapters explore the changing role of the manager and draw a distinction between managing and leading, which provides an important framework as you navigate these *"power10"* waters.

2. Begin with the overall assessment

Once you have read the chapters that cover managing and leading, it's time to embark on the chapter entitled "Overall Effectiveness." This chapter has you complete the *"power10"* overall assessment. Results from the assessment pinpoint which *"power10"* success factors need the most focus and action.

Who will you have participate in the assessment process?

- Individual teams
- Departments
- Management and leadership teams
- Everyone in the organization

Generally team members will assess their own team, but you may choose to have them assess the department as a whole. Or you may choose to have management and leadership teams assess their team or the entire organization.

3. Focus on the two or three "power10" success factors that need the most work

As you continue your *"power10"* journey, you will explore the chapters for the two to three success factors needing the most work. These drill-down assessments will help you understand what contributes to where your team or organization sees itself today. The results provide insights that will make developing plans and actions much easier and more focused.

4. Develop actions

Now that the priorities have been identified, it's time for you and your crew to develop plans to address the *"power10" success factors* requiring the most focus and attention.

5. Call for a "power10"

With the plans developed, it's time to call for a *"power10."* You need your crew to give ten of their best, perfectly timed, most powerful strokes to successfully navigate the waters to improve their effectiveness.

6. Celebrate success!

Be sure to celebrate the progress and success along the way. People want to make a difference and feel recognized and appreciated for their contributions to success.

Each *"power10"* success factor has its own chapter, which you may also use as a stand-alone resource. Chapters include an overview, a self-assessment, practical tools, and insights and tips to navigate the waters of change. These items can be used to help the crew, as it prepares and executes its plan to increase effectiveness and improve performance. But again, I believe you will gain the greatest benefit if you begin with the chapters "On Managing and Leading" and "Your Leadership Role" and complete the *Overall Effectiveness Self-Assessment* before proceeding to the other chapters.

Many of the actions that are taken will have a residual effect, positively impacting other areas of the business. You will find similar messages in more than one chapter of *"power10" Leadership,* due to the relationship of various success factors. In addition, you will notice a number of situational statements that reside in more than one chapter's self-assessment.

Download digital templates and tools

You will find a wide variety of templates and tools throughout *"power10" Leadership* designed to make your job easier. To access an electronic version of the available tools, simply go to www.businespaths.net, click on the power10 link, register and enter password: power10. Then download the digital files you want to use.

Let "power10" Leadership show you where to focus your time and attention! And, get ready to call for a "power10"!

On Managing and Leading

Are you the manager and leader you want to be?

Thousands of books and courses have been offered that provide insights into how to perform successfully in management and leadership roles. Nevertheless, I have worked with hundreds of people in management positions over the years and have only found a handful of them who feel they've mastered the level of expertise they hoped to.

Most admit that they allow day-to-day pressures that nip at their heels to take priority. Others recognize that while many of the books they've read and classes they've attended ignited their interest and passion, most focused on concept and theory, rather than methods for implementing the powerful insights offered.

As a manager and leader, you have a lot on your plate. And my guess is that you need someone, as I did, to develop the methods and tools for improving your personal effectiveness, as well as that of your team and organization.

This is precisely why I have written this book.

As you read in the chapter "How to Use This Book," *"power10" Leadership* focuses on ten *"power10"* success factors. It asks you to complete self-assessments to pinpoint those things that work well on your team or in your organization and identify those critical few areas that need additional focus and action. In addition to the assessments, you will find *"power10" Leadership* filled with valuable insights, practical tools and sound advice.

Before you set out to explore *"power10" Leadership,* I would like to offer the following insights into managing and leading. They will serve as a framework for your successful journey.

Insights into managing and leading

Over the past several decades, management and leadership roles have changed significantly in response to our fast-paced, ever-changing business environment. In order to compete, organizations have become flatter, and decision-making has moved closer to the customer. Self-directed teams have been formed, and the need for leadership at all levels has come into focus. As a result, roles throughout the organization have changed.

For example strategic thinking and planning, and partnering with suppliers and vendors, responsibilities once held at the executive level, now involve people occupying the management ranks. Attending to the day-to-day business, solving problems, and finding innovative ways to improve how to approach the work and achieve success has shifted to front-line employees. This shift in responsibility drives the need for increased leadership and decision-making at all levels of the organization and involves you knowing when to manage and when to lead.

The difference between managing and leading

Peter F. Drucker, internationally renowned pioneer in Social and Management Theory, described the difference between managing and leading in the following way:

"Management is doing things right: leadership is doing the right things."

So, what does that really mean? Over time, the role of the manager has changed from telling people what to do and how to do it, to sharing the direction for the team or organization and actively engaging people in determining how to get there. This change has driven the need to empower employees to make decisions, solve problems, and run the day-to-day business.

As a result, developing leaders at all levels has become an important part of addressing changing business needs and reflects the vital role that people throughout the organization play in achieving organizational success. This shift, coupled with the advent of self-directed work teams, demands that managers spend more of their time leading and less time managing.

These shifts in responsibility have driven significant cultural change for many organizations. Management and leadership styles have had to change from one of *command and control* to one of *participation and empowerment*. This has meant difficult times for many people in management positions. Those managers who were unable to adapt to this new environment joined a list of casualties.

Many experts have worked to clarify the difference between managing and leading. Warren Bennis in his book *On Becoming a Leader* points out significant differences between managing and leading. He contrasts those differences using the two themes of Peter Drucker: 1) *focusing on doing things right* and 2) *doing the right thing*. But, his bottom line states:

You need to lead people and manage things.

Where you focus your attention and action will drive the performance and success of your team and organization. And, when you recognize when you are managing and when you are leading, you can consciously choose to invest your time in activities that are appropriate for a given situation. Let's take a closer look at managing and leading.

A closer look at managing...

Many people in management positions have been taught to manage, not to lead. They grew up in organizations where *command and control* management styles were the norm. In this environment, managers told people what to do and how to do it. Then, if something went wrong, the employees believed it was the managers' problem because they made the decisions and gave the marching orders.

A command and control management approach tends to create a dependence on management and provides a reasonably "safe," risk-averse environment for employees. It involves centralized decision-making, one-way, top-down communication and limited employee empowerment.

In the *command and control* environment, managers generally expect implementation and compliance from their people. This approach includes:

- Directing and performing activities
- Following prescribed procedures
- Doing what is asked
- Ensuring agreements are met
- Functioning within boundaries

It typically does not leave room for creativity and innovation in people's approach to their work and success.

Employees find this management style manipulative, restrictive, stifling, and rigid. And they do not respond well to this management approach.

A closer look at leading...

There has been much written on leadership. Here are a few experts' definitions:

"Leadership is influence—nothing more, nothing less," says John Maxwell, an internationally recognized leadership expert, speaker, and author.

"Leaders help ordinary people achieve extraordinary results," says Ken Blanchard, one of the most influential leadership experts in the world.

Warren Bennis, one of the nation's foremost authorities on organizational development, leadership, and change may be closer to reality when he says, "Leadership is like beauty; it's hard to define, but you know it when you see it."

Though their definitions may vary slightly, experts embrace a common theme: They recognize the valuable role the people play in achieving organizational success. And participative leadership and empowerment pave the way for getting everyone in the boat rowing the same direction.

In this environment, you will find people in management positions focused on:

- Identifying new ways of doing things
- Making improvements
- Planning for the future
- Engaging others to take action
- Building relationships and trust

They actively develop people, encourage innovation and risk taking, and ensure a team and process focus.

This shift in role requires a new set of skills...skills for engaging people in the development of strategies, empowering them to work together to run the day-to-day business, and enabling them find new and innovative ways to approach the business and deliver results. In this new environment, managers need to know how to negotiate and collaborate. They need to learn how to empower their people, as well as hold them accountable for delivering results. As you can see, the managers' role changes and evolves requiring them to function in more of a leadership role. They become change agents, communicators, coaches and facilitators.

When you embrace participative leadership and empowerment, you will tap into your people's knowledge and experience, unleash their creativity, and engage them in running the day-to-day business. Employees find this leadership approach enabling, freeing, flexible, and democratic. As a result, they feel challenged, willingly take some risks, and appreciate feeling trusted to do the right thing.

A reflection:

During my corporate years, I remember directives that came down from headquarters or the region for implementation. And, though the intent of the people who developed the 'whats' and 'hows' was honorable, the 'hows' assumed that every team, department, and organization were the same.

A frequent reaction from the people in the field was, "How they are telling us to do this simply won't work." The result of this approach left people in the field believing that the folks in headquarters and the region office were out of touch with what was happening where "the rubber meets the road." Though some directives allowed for flexibility during implementation, many were expected to be followed to the letter.

Then, as the business climate changed, the company went through a major cultural revolution. Differences across the organization were acknowledged, a participative approach was introduced, and local teams were empowered to determine how best to support the new directives and programs that came down the pike. This approach was a win-win because the company got what it needed, and teams and departments took ownership and gained commitment to making the programs a success.

Both managing and leading should be at the top of your list of important responsibilities. How much time you invest in each activity depends on the situation at hand. However, you should expect to spend more time leading, and expect the people working for you to invest more time managing activities that you used to handle. In his book, *Leading Change*, John Kotter, Harvard Business School Professor, widely regarded as the world's foremost authority on leadership and change, points out that, during times of change, managers should be spending 70 - 90 percent of their time leading and 20–30 percent managing. And I haven't found a manager or leader yet who doesn't believe they are dealing with constant change.

Key Differences between Managing and Leading

As you balance the need for *doing things right* and *doing the right things*, you will shift from focusing on the 'how-tos,' and working on 'the now,' to focusing more on the 'whats' and 'whys,' building relationships and trust, and planning for the future.

Managing:	Leading:
• Is more tactical in nature	• Is more strategic
• Leans toward compliance and implementation	• Is focused on innovation and change
• Promotes individual contribution	• Embraces inclusion and development

And, remember Warren Bennis' important bottom line:

You need to manage things and lead people

Please do not underestimate the significance of this shift in role for the people in management positions. Those who are reluctant or unable to adapt to this new environment pave the way for a new set of leaders to emerge. These new leaders set the pace and tone, motivate their people, create and develop work teams, and manage a process that consistently delivers results.

Why embracing this change is so important:

In today's fast-paced, competitive environment, organizations need to attract and retain the best and the brightest people to help shape the future. And today's employees want to work where:

- They feel a part of an organization
- Trust is the glue that holds it all together
- They have pride in the organization they are a part of
- They know they can make a difference
- They can have an influence over their future
- They feel appreciated for their contributions

The only way you will get everyone in the boat rowing the same direction is to recognize and embrace the fact that your people are your most valuable asset. The old ways of interacting and behaving simply don't work anymore. You must lead and develop your people to be the best they can be in order to shape both the success of your team and future of your organization.

Take stock of where you invest your time

Most of the managers and leaders I have worked with struggle to find enough hours in a day to do everything they need to do to be highly successful. How you invest your available time will determine whether you work 40 - 50 hour weeks or 60 - 70 hour weeks. It will also influence how productive your team or organization is.

According to the World Confederation of Productivity Science research, the average American business wastes or misdirects work time as follows:

- 23 percent waiting for approvals, materials, or support
- 20 percent doing things that shouldn't even be done
- 15 percent doing things that should be handled by someone else
- 18 percent doing things wrong
- 16 percent failing to do the right things

Do you find yourself caught up in any of these time-wasting activities?

We've covered the difference between managing and leading and recognize that current circumstance will determine how much time you spend in each area. We've also covered the importance of spending more time leading. But, in addition to the time you spend managing and leading, you may find yourself involved in a third activity that robs valuable time.

"Doing" activities can consume valuable time unnecessarily. Why? Because you probably should not be doing them in the first place. It's easy to fall into this trap because:

- You are comfortable doing them
- You may have excelled at them in previous positions
- You think it's easier to do it yourself than try to get someone else to do it

---

"Doing" can be a time robber!

If you are a *working manager,* you will find yourself involved in more "doing" activities because you have individual responsibility for delivering a specific piece of the business.

Take a few minutes to think through activities you regularly perform and which category they fall into: leading people, managing things, or doing other people's activities. List them below.

Leading People	**Managing Things**	**Doing Others Activities**
Examples: Setting clear direction, defining empowerments, providing coaching and feedback, etc.	*Examples: Approving time reporting, reviewing performance trends, writing performance appraisals, etc.*	*Examples: Researching the cause of a work-team problem, typing a report your aide should be typing, etc.*
70-90% *during times of change*	**20-30%** *during times of change*	*0% Transition them to the person responsible.*

Review your list and make conscious decisions about where to invest your time to capture the greatest payback. Identify managing activities that can be shifted to people who report to you, and shift doing activities to the person(s) responsible for their completion. This will allow you to accomplish more, increase empowerment and improve the quality and effectiveness of your work.

On Managing and Leading

Insights:	Tips:
<ul><li>There are major differences between managing and leading.</li><li>The role of the manager has changed significantly.</li><li>Managing focuses on doing things right.</li><li>Leading focuses on doing the right things.</li><li>Both managing and leading are important.</li><li>More leadership is required today.</li><li>During times of change 70-90% of your time should be spent leading.</li><li>Not all managers are equipped to make the transition.</li></ul>	<ul><li>Lead more, manage less.</li><li>Choose where to invest your time.</li><li>Be sure to lead people and manage things.</li><li>Engage your people in running the day-to-day business.</li><li>Transition "doing" activities to the people responsible for them.</li></ul>

For information about available products and services visit www.businesspaths.net

Your Leadership Role

Leading people

Just as the Coxswain is responsible for keeping the boat on the most direct course, motivating the rowers and serving as the on-the-water coach, you are the leader of your team or organization. You each have responsibility for setting the pace and tone, motivating your people, and providing the coaching that will deliver the best performance. Your leadership style and approach will have a significant impact on your team and organization's success.

You will find a variety of leadership styles out there. Some have subtle differences, others much sharper contrast. Let's take a look at a few of them:

Transformational Leadership was originally introduced in a 1947 model by German psychologist and political economist Max Weber, and reintroduced in 1978 by presidential biographer and authority on leadership studies, James MacGregor Burns. Transformational leadership creates valuable and positive change in the followers. A transformational leader focuses on "transforming" others to help each other, to look out for each other, to be encouraging and harmonious, and to look out for the organization as a whole. In this style of leadership, the leader enhances the motivation, morale, and performance of his or her follower group.

Servant Leadership coined in 1964 by Robert Greenleaf, founder of the Servant Leadership movement, has leaders achieving results for the organization by giving priority attention to the needs of their colleagues and those they serve. Servant-leaders are often seen as humble stewards of their organization's resources (human, financial, and physical).

Participative Leadership, also known as democratic leadership, was introduced in 1939 by German-American psychologist Kurt Lewin. Participative leadership takes a consultative management approach that encourages others to participate. Leadership decisions are achieved as the end result of group participation. Leaders involve subordinates in goal setting, problem solving, team building, etc.

Situational Leadership was introduced by behavioral scientists and entrepreneurs Paul Hersey and Ken Blanchard, author of *The One Minute Manager*, and management expert. It can be found in the first edition of *Management of Organizational Behavior*, introduced in the 1960s. It suggests that there is no single best style...that leaders need to adapt by choosing a directing, coaching, supporting, or delegating approach based on a given situation.

Transactional Leadership was originally introduced in a 1947 model by Max Weber and reintroduced in contrast to transformational leadership by James MacGregor Burns in 1978. Transactional leaders believe that people are motivated by reward or punishment. A transactional leader focuses more on a series of "transactions." These leaders give clear instructions to followers about what their expectations are. When those expectations are fulfilled there are rewards in store and failure is severely punished. They allocate work to subordinates whether resources are there or absent.

Whether you subscribe to one or more of these leadership concepts, the role you play as the leader is critical to success. Please note that most of these styles place a high level of importance on those who actually perform the work. The people who report to you are your most valuable asset, because it is through them that you will succeed.

What's happening in reality?

In a 2006 Ken Blanchard Companies' study of more than 1400 managers, leaders, and executives, participants identified the following five things that leaders most often fail to do when working with others:

- *82 percent fail to provide appropriate feedback*
- *81 percent fail to listen or involve others in the process*
- *76 percent fail to use a leadership style that is appropriate to the person, task, or situation*
- *76 percent fail to set clear goals and objectives*
- *59 percent fail to train and develop their people*

Having spent the majority of my adult life in management and leadership roles, and over a decade as a management consultant, my experience also supports these findings.

How can leaders hope to get everyone in the boat rowing the same direction with ratings like this? They can't. There are clearly opportunities for leaders to perform more effectively in their roles.

The effectiveness of the leadership role you play will have a significant impact on team and organizational success. It will also have a lasting impact on the lives and livelihood of every person that works with and for you.

How effectively do leaders in your organization function in their role?

Focus on your primary customer

Every organization that provides products or services recognizes that their primary external customers are those who purchase their product or service.

Not all managers realize that their primary internal customers, however, are the people who report directly to them…their most valuable asset…those who need their outputs, information, or support to do their job.

Your people represent the primary face and voice to the external customer. They process customer requests and solve customer problems. They are the ones who build customer confidence and trust in the organization. They are there because you single handedly cannot accomplish all the work yourself. If you could, there would be no need for their jobs to exist.

So, how do you ensure that your people serve the customer well and deliver the performance that is required? You develop them to be the best they can be. Your people will thrive when you give them the opportunity to learn and grow. It is through expectation-setting, training, empowerment, coaching, and feedback that your people will become the best they can be. It is important that you fully embrace this concept and actively develop your people to reap the rewards. Without knowledgeable, highly-skilled people, sustainable performance will be out of reach.

A leadership story

I fondly remember leading teams and organizations throughout my management career. It seemed like my assignments often involved working with groups of people who were struggling and had not enjoyed the thrill of success. It was clear that I needed to dig deep into my leadership tool kit to find ways to support the effort. I needed to find the patience and persistence and muster an undying commitment to build a team or organization that could pull together, navigate the prevailing waters, move across the finish line, and eventually end up on the medal stand.

Luckily, the organization's environment was shifting from command-and-control to one of participation and empowerment. And I believed that, if I could get everyone in the boat rowing the same direction, rather than the boat going around in circles, with people jumping or being thrown overboard, we could accomplish anything.

Working with the belief that people want to do a good job, I assessed the situation and set clear direction. During my information-gathering phase, it became clear that people really wanted to be part of a successful team and organization. But they needed help and encouragement to make it happen. My job was to get them the support they needed to deliver what was expected and ensure that they received regular feedback on how they were doing against expectations.

It was always exciting to see the progress that was being made. People started feeling like there was hope; they believed that there was light at the end of the tunnel, and it wasn't a train coming toward them. You could feel the stress lifting. People were feeling better about themselves and what the team and organization were able to accomplish. They could tell we were on course and headed toward the finish line.

That is not to say we didn't encounter white water while on our journey. There were people who didn't want things to change, because they were more comfortable doing them the way they had always been done. Other people openly challenged the direction we were headed, often to mask their personal insecurity. They didn't know if they could function effectively in this new environment. Those who wouldn't or couldn't get in the boat and row the same direction became the casualties of progress.

I'm reminded of a saying: *Success breeds success.* I've found it to be very true. When you bring people together, set the pace and tone, get them focused on a common purpose, and support the heck out of them and their efforts, "magic" can happen. And when you recognize progress and success along the way, it builds confidence. Once people have a taste of success, they will work hard and long to continue to enjoy the thrill.

What do your primary internal customers need from you?

Everyone needs leadership, and your people need and expect it from you, their manager. There are things they want, they need, and they expect. So, take a few minutes to think through and answer the following question:

What do your primary internal customers (the people who report directly to you) want, need, and expect?

Want:	Need:	Expect:
*Example: To enjoy getting up and coming to work every day**	*Example: To feel like they can make a difference**	*Example: To be treated fairly and equitably**
*Example: To be successful**	*Example: To have clear direction and expectations**	*Example: To receive open, honest feedback**
Example: To feel valued	*Example: To know their manager appreciates their hard work*	*Example: To receive positive reinforcement for a job well done*

Place an asterisk (*) next to the wants, needs, and expectations that you, as their manager, either influence or directly impact.

Now, ask yourself, *"How consistently, and by what means, do I meet their requirements?"*

Jot down the things you do today to support their requirements. Then enter those things that you need to start doing to respond to your people's needs.

What I do today to meet their requirements:	What I need to start doing to meet their requirements:
Example: Meet with each person monthly to talk about his or her contributions and performance.	*Example: Implement a formal performance and evaluation process.*
	Example: Find people in the act of doing things right.
	Now, add these to your personal development plan.

What is Your Most Important Skill?

Review what you just identified that your people need from you, what you do today to meet their requirements, and what you need to start doing to meet their requirements. What skill will you use the most to meet their requirements?

_____

(most important skill)

Whether your people need direction, your time, motivation, clarity, honesty, understanding, etc., the primary skill you use is communication. Think about it. Communication serves as the basis for:

- Setting expectations
- Discussing problems and potential solutions
- Providing coaching

- Conducting meetings
- Sharing feedback
- Recognizing performance contributions

Let's take a look at how a Ken Blanchard Group study of more 1400 leaders, managers, and executives felt about leadership communication:

- 43 percent of the respondents felt that communicating and listening were the most critical skills of a leader, and

- 41 percent felt that inappropriate use of communication or listening was the biggest mistake leaders make

My years of consulting confirm these results. The greatest challenge the majority of organizations, departments, and teams face is effective communication. With communication being such an integral part of our lives, why does it pose so many challenges?

Most leaders are uncomfortable "saying the words."

They fear hurting someone's feelings, causing conflict, or generating an emotional response. But, how can you help your people become the best they can be, if you are unwilling to talk openly about areas they need to improve? How can you provide the teaching and coaching necessary to assist with their growth? How can you provide feedback on their development? You have got to speak openly and honestly to develop your people to be the best they can be.

Another major reason communication poses such a challenge for many leaders is the absence of a communication plan. They have not developed a method for ensuring regular, ongoing, and consistent communication, which is the basis for building relationships and trust.

Whose responsibility is it?

As a leader, you are ultimately responsible for everything that happens or doesn't happen on your team or in your organization. At times, it is difficult for some managers to get their heads around this concept, but it is true.

When problems surface in your organization or on your team, i.e., performance shortfalls, conflict, infighting, etc., It is a LEADERSHIP issue

---

Let me repeat…It is a *leadership* issue… perhaps the result of unclear direction, the need for role clarity, a lack of training, etc. When you review your group's performance and observe their behaviors, what you see is your reflection in a mirror…a direct reflection of the quality of your leadership. Harsh? Maybe so. But true.

If you want to attract and retain the best and the brightest people to move the organization into the future, you must function effectively in your leadership role and create an environment where your people feel like part of an organization:

> …Where trust is the glue that holds it all together
> …Where they have pride in the organization they are a part of
> …Where they know they can make a difference
> …Where they can have an influence over their future
> …Where they feel appreciated for their contributions

When you have…

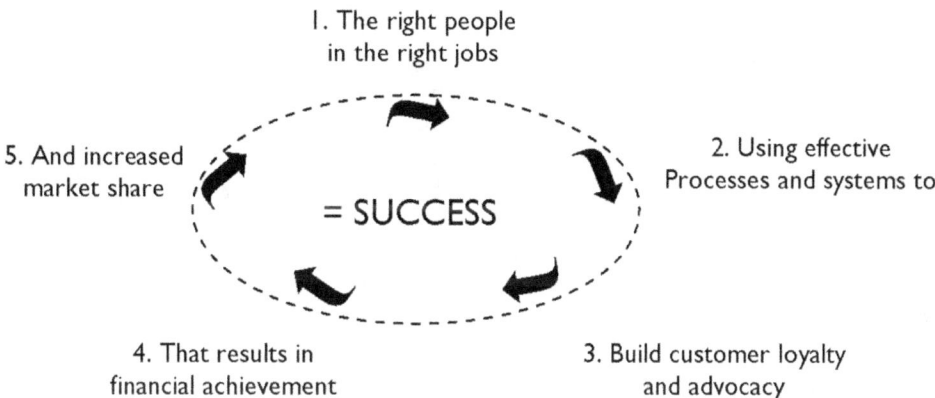

1. The right people in the right jobs
2. Using effective Processes and systems to
3. Build customer loyalty and advocacy
4. That results in financial achievement
5. And increased market share
= SUCCESS

In summary

The only way to get everyone in the boat rowing the same direction is to recognize and embrace the fact that your people are your most valuable asset. The old ways of interacting and behaving simply don't work anymore. You must lead and develop your people to be the best they can be. In this way, you will shape the future for your team or organization.

On Your Leadership Role:

Insights:

- Your most valuable asset: Your people
- Your top priority: Your primary external and internal customers
- Your primary internal customers: Those who report directly to you
- Most leaders are uncomfortable "saying the words".
- Communication is your most important skill

Tips:

- Strive for excellence
- Always remember…people want to do a good job
- Know what your people want, need and expect from you.
- Execute well
- Communicate openly and honestly
- Focus on doing the right things
- Build relationships and trust

For information about available products and services visit www.businesspaths.net

Overall Effectiveness

How effective is your team or organization?

In today's environment, organizations face demands on both time and resources. Competitive pressures and financial tightening finds organizations searching for ways to do more with less. With labor being the single largest organizational expense, improving overall effectiveness becomes vital. When organizations redirect their people's time and energy to more value-added work, they gain the flexibility and productivity needed to meet changing customer requirements, support employee needs, and achieve financial objectives.

One of your organization's top priorities has got to be its external customers. Without them, there would be no reason to exist. Customers want to do business with organizations that have a solid reputation and are easy to do business with. They also expect to receive quality products and relevant services. Customers want businesses to respond to their needs and solve problems to their satisfaction in a timely manner.

Unfortunately, few organizations today consistently meet these customer expectations.

Understanding and responding to what your internal customers need also plays a significant role in increasing overall effectiveness. Your employees want to be part of a winning organization, where they can learn and grow and be treated fairly. They want to know how they can make a difference, have influence over their future, and feel valued for their contributions.

Unfortunately, typically less than five percent of employees know the direction their organization is heading, and less than one third are truly engaged at work. In order to get everyone in the boat rowing the same direction, employees need to understand what the organization is striving to accomplish and how they can contribute. Showing up to simply get a paycheck needs to be replaced with active involvement and commitment to delivering results and achieving success.

How effectively does your organization...

- Attract and retain the best and the brightest people?
- Create an environment that promotes success?
- Respond to changing customer requirements and organizational needs?
- Achieve measurable, sustainable results?
- Position itself for the future?

What can you do to increase overall effectiveness?

Leaders and managers have responsibility for maximizing the overall effectiveness of the organization. They need to:

1) Source, hire, and develop the best and brightest
2) Clarify and communicate key priorities
3) Engage people in developing and taking actions that support achievement of the priorities, and
4) Manage a process that ensures that the team and organization deliver the desired results

Management must ensure that they have the right people in the right jobs. They also need to ensure that their people consistently utilize effective processes and systems to respond to changing customer and business needs. It takes a proactive approach to running the business to ensure that the organization delivers performance, achieves financial results, and positions itself for the future.

A couple of questions that people in management positions often ask, as they strive to do more with less, are *"How can we increase our overall effectiveness?,"* and *"Where do we start?"*

It begins with you embracing the fact that your people are your most valuable asset. And, if your goal is to ensure consistently strong performance, when you work with and make things happen through your people, the team and organization will succeed.

Managers and leaders have responsibility for developing their people to be the best they can be.

When you tap into your people's creativity and engage them in running the business, they thrive. They will accomplish extraordinary things when armed with the knowledge, information, tools, and support to do the job.

To get everyone in the boat rowing the same direction, begin with setting clear direction. Then ensure that you foster open communication and engage employees in running the day-to-day business. As you empower your people to solve problems and find new and innovative ways to address customer and organizational needs, your team or organization will gain a deeper understanding of the business and what it takes to achieve success.

Over time, relationships deepen and people share information and knowledge. As a result, trust builds, allowing everyone to come together, row in the same direction, and collectively achieve team and organizational success.

The opportunity for continuous learning and growth and having people feel valued for their contributions is vital for attracting and retaining quality people. Through the development of teams and partnerships, you create a synergy that leads to success in today's highly competitive, dynamic environment.

Examine your organization or team's overall effectiveness

Take a few minutes to complete the following overall effectiveness self-assessment.

First, decide which group you will assess. The organization? A department? A team? Now, keep this group *top of mind* as you proceed through the self-assessment. Your ratings will identify conditions that contribute to the group's effectiveness and pinpoint areas that need additional focus and attention.

The Self-Assessment includes ten pairs of statements representing factors that contribute to organizational effectiveness. Read the statement in the left-hand and right-hand column for each "power10" success factor. Place an "x" on the scale of one to seven that indicates where you view the team, department, or organization *today* in relationship to the two statements. If you find that part of the description rates higher and part lower, plot the lower rating on the scale of one to seven.

Here is an example of one pair of statements and the rating scale:

"power10" SUCCESS FACTOR:	WHERE WE ARE	WHERE WE NEED TO BE
Common Purpose: Direction, priorities, and roles are unclear; focus is on short-term action with little regard for long-term impacts.	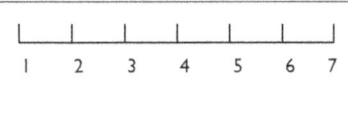	**Common Purpose:** Strategic direction, clear priorities, and associated roles and responsibilities are developed and well understood.

If you decide to have multiple people participate in the self-assessment process, keep this in mind:

People generally believe that their team or organization falls into a high-performing category. However, when I have facilitated the self-assessment process, I've noticed that, as groups review the summary of their individual ratings, they are astonished to find they've rated themselves extremely low. They even suggest that they must have been thinking about the organization when they applied the rating—certainly not their team.

When this situation became a barrier to moving forward with plans and actions to improve the team's effectiveness, I had them retake the self-assessment, being sure to focus on their team or group. In every situation, the overall ratings came out the same or lower than the original assessment.

The moral of the story:

- Ensure everyone participating in the self-assessment is clear about which group he or she is assessing.

- Assure everyone that the overall assessment simply provides a starting point for developing plans and implementing actions that will increase the team or group's effectiveness.

If participants tell you, "It's tough settling on a rating," it's likely they feel that the group does well against some parts of the description and not so well against others. As a result, they have a tough time assigning a rating. Share the following example, which will help them feel more comfortable applying a rating.

> As you read the statements in the left-hand and right-hand columns, let's say you believe that priorities are pretty well defined and communicated throughout the organization (a 6 rating), but a formal Strategic Plan does not exist (a 3 rating). Confusion about roles and responsibilities and who makes which decisions surfaces regularly (a 2 rating). Though the organization does a good job of addressing the day-to-day operations, you would like to see a better balance between short-term and long-term focus and action (a 3 rating). You just came up with one 2, two 3s, and one 6 rating.

> As you select an overall rating for this "power10" success factor, "err on the low side" to ensure that areas receiving 2 and 3 ratings get addressed. In this example, you may choose to give Common Purpose an overall rating of 2.5.

Now, take a few minutes to complete the "power10" overall effectiveness assessment on the following page for your organization, department or team.

Overall Effectiveness Assessment for: _____

(i.e. ABC Company, Sales Department, Financial Team)

Read the statements in the left-hand and right-hand columns for each of the "power10" success factors. Place an "x" on the scale of one to seven that indicates where you view the team, department, or organization *today* in relationship to the two statements.

"power10" SUCCESS FACTOR:	WHERE WE ARE	WHERE WE NEED TO BE
Common Purpose: Direction, priorities, and roles are unclear; focus is on short-term actions with little regard for long-term impacts.	1 2 3 4 5 6 7	**Common Purpose:** Strategic direction, clear priorities, and associated roles and responsibilities are developed and well understood
Performance Management: There are inconsistencies in how performance is reviewed or little understanding of where focus and improvement are needed.	1 2 3 4 5 6 7	**Performance Management:** Performance is reviewed on a regular basis to celebrate accomplishments and identify areas requiring continued focus and improvement.
Delegation and Empowerment: Decisions are made at management levels and shared with members for implementation.	1 2 3 4 5 6 7	**Delegation and Empowerment:** Members are actively involved in making decisions that affect their work, and they take full responsibility and accountability for the outcomes.
Problem Solving: Problems are addressed and decisions are made independently or in an unstructured manner.	1 2 3 4 5 6 7	**Problem Solving:** Members share responsibility for addressing problems and selecting solutions utilizing a disciplined, fact-based approach.
Continuous Improvement: Multiple priorities leave little time to focus on ways to improve how the work is done.	1 2 3 4 5 6 7	**Continuous Improvement:** Members consistently look for new and innovative ways to improve the quality of products and services and how the work is done.
Communication: Communication is guarded, resulting in minimal involvement in addressing and resolving issues.	1 2 3 4 5 6 7	**Communication:** A high level of openness and honesty allows members to share information, ideas, and opinions to address and resolve issues.
Learning and Growth: Members are protective of individual knowledge and are reluctant to share their expertise with others.	1 2 3 4 5 6 7	**Learning and Growth:** There is a strong commitment to continuous learning and knowledge sharing to enhance overall effectiveness.
Team Development: There is internal competition, individual contributor focus, and few joint efforts to improve how the team(s) operate.	1 2 3 4 5 6 7	**Team Development:** There is a spirit of cooperation that enables collaborative efforts to improve how the team(s) operate and how results are achieved.
Environment: There is little trust established, which results in conflict and win-lose outcomes.	1 2 3 4 5 6 7	**Environment:** There is a high level of trust and mutual respect that allows members to feel valued for their contributions, and win-win outcomes to be achieved.
Results: Performance results are sporadic, which negatively impact confidence and morale of members.	1 2 3 4 5 6 7	**Results:** Desired results are consistently delivered, with members being recognized for their contributions and achievements.

Where does your organization or team need to focus?

To pinpoint which factors need the most work to strengthen overall effectiveness, review your assessment and enter the three highest-rated and lowest-rated factors below.

Which three "power10" Success Factors did you rate the highest (closest to seven) on the overall assessment?	Which three "power10" Success Factors did you rate the lowest (closest to one) on the overall assessment?
1.	1.
2.	2.
3.	3.

Next Steps

- For those "power10" success factors rated the highest on the overall assessment, keep doing what you are doing.
- For those "power10" success factors rated the lowest on the overall assessment, see "What's contributing to your 'power10' assessment."

Note: If you completed the assessment on your own and found value in this exercise, consider expanding the self-assessment to include other members of the organization or team. For example:

1. Have the Executive Team complete the self-assessment on the organization.
2. Have all team members complete the self-assessment on the department.

Expanding involvement provides additional insights, commitment, and support, which contribute to the common purpose of the organization.

If you have multiple teams or departments that you would like to participate in the self-assessment process, contact us at www.businesspaths.net to learn more about our on-line assessment services.

What's contributing to your "power10" assessment?

Just as the overall assessment helped you identify the three areas needing the most work, the drill-down assessments will help you identify the lowest rated contributing factors. Go to the respective chapters for the three *"power10" Success Factors* you rated the lowest, read the chapter and complete the self-assessment for each of them now. Then enter your findings on the worksheet that follows.

You will find drill-down assessments for "power10" success factors you rated the lowest in their respective chapters:

Contributors to the lowest-rated "power10" success factors:

Lowest-Rated *"power10"* Success Factor: _____
(i.e. Common Purpose, Communication, etc.)

Three Lowest-Rated Contributing Factors:	Where We Are Today: (Your or the participating groups' assessment)	Where We Need To Be: (Pulled from the Self-Assessment right hand column)
1)		
2)		
3)		

Second Lowest-Rated *"power10"* Success Factor: _____
(i.e. Common Purpose, Communication, etc.)

Three Lowest-Rated Contributing Factors:	Where We Are Today: (Your or the participating groups' assessment)	Where We Need To Be: (Pulled from the Self-Assessment right hand column)
1)		
2)		
3)		

Third Lowest-Rated *"power10"* Success Factor: _____
(i.e. Common Purpose, Communication, etc.)

Three Lowest-Rated Contributing Factors:	Where We Are Today: (Your or the participating groups' assessment)	Where We Need To Be: (Pulled from the Self-Assessment right hand column)
1)		
2)		
3)		

Contributors to the lowest-rated "power10" success factors – EXAMPLE:

Three Lowest-Rated Contributing Factors:	Where We Are Today: (Your or the participating groups' assessment)	Where We Need To Be: (Pulled from the Self-Assessment)
1) Mission	There is not a defined Mission for the organization.	The group's over-riding purpose is well defined and regularly used to guide decisions and actions.
2) Goals and Objectives	Some areas have established goals, but there is an opportunity to align them with organizational goals.	There are established goals and objectives that members actively focus on achieving.
3) Measures	There is an absence of metrics throughout the organization.	Measures are applied and regularly utilized to monitor progress and gauge success.
Three Lowest-Rated Contributing Factors:	Where We Are Today: (Your or the participating groups' assessment)	Where We Need To Be: (Pulled from the Self-Assessment)
1) Expectations	There is not a consistent process for setting expectations throughout the organization.	There is a clear set of performance expectations, with associated measures that are aligned with the overall direction.
2) Coaching	Managers and Supervisors provide coaching to their people as the need arises.	Ongoing coaching and feedback are provided to enhance knowledge and develop skills to improve performance.
3) Accountability	We don't have a sound process for holding people accountable for their performance contributions.	Members are held accountable for delivering desired performance results.
Three Lowest-Rated Contributing Factors:	Where We Are Today: (Your or the participating groups' assessment)	Where We Need To Be: (Pulled from the Self-Assessment)
1) Management Information	There is an absence of metrics to build a Management Information System around.	There is a comprehensive MIS that accurately reflects current performance trends and ongoing results.
2) Tracking and Monitoring	There is an absence of metrics to provide the basis for tracking progress and success.	Effective methods for tracking progress and monitoring results are in place and regularly utilized as the basis for accountability.
3) Reward and Recognition	There is not a defined recognition plan in place.	Formal and informal recognition plans are in place to provide individual and team reward and recognition.

With the two to three *"power10" success factors* identified that need the most work, and details from the drill-down reflecting what contributed to the ratings, you have a sound basis for healthy discussion, plan development, and action.

Take Action—Call for a "power10"!

Now it's time to move to the plans and actions phase. You will find an action document on page 45 of this chapter for your use. During action planning, you will identify specific actions, assign responsibility, and establish due dates. The action plan will then become a working document for conducting status updates.

Once the action plan is complete, schedule regular meetings with the individuals assigned responsibility for overseeing specific actions. My recommendation would be to initially meet on a monthly basis. Those people assigned responsibility should come prepared to provide a status and report on the progress and success of their assigned actions.

Be sure to celebrate the progress that is being made and the success that is being achieved, as a result of the plans and actions. People want to be part of a winning organization and feel appreciated for their contributions to the success of the team or organization.

Overall Effectiveness	
Insights:	**Tips:**
• The organization and team's most valuable asset is their people. • People want to be part of a winning organization. • Typically <5% of employees know where the organization is going. • Less than 1/3 of employees are truly engaged at work. • By prioritizing the critical few areas that need work, you can focus plans and actions to improve your team or organization's effectiveness.	• Customers should be treated as the top priority. • People who report directly to you are your most important internal customers. • Develop your people to be the best they can be. • Create an environment that attracts and retains the best and brightest. • Focus on the critical few priorities. • Get everyone in the boat rowing the same direction.

For information about available products and services visit www.businesspaths.net

Commitment to Action

Key Focus Area: _____

Future State/Goal: _____

Agreed Upon Action(s)	Responsible Person(s)	Planned/ Actual Completion	Measure(s)	Status:

Commitment to Action – EXAMPLE

Key Focus Area: *A Training/Resource Information Center*

Future State/Goal: *Ensure that Quality Assurance is the primary resource used for achieving a common understanding of conformity and compliance requirements throughout the organization*

Agreed Upon Action(s)	Responsible Person(s)	Planned/ Actual Completion	Measure(s)	Status:
Establish and document Quality Assurance roles, responsibilities, and expectations	Director of QA + task force	10/31	Three components are documented	
Develop a presentation for cascading QA support services	Task force	11/15	Presentation is finalized	
Communicate QA services to all Associates	QA Lead	12/31	All Associates are familiar with QA services	
Develop a training plan to ensure all QA Associates are up to speed with their roles and responsibilities	Task force	12/1	Training plan is complete	
Train needed QA Associates	QA Lead	12/31	Required training is complete	

Common Purpose

Get everyone in the boat rowing the same direction

In the world of rowing, as the season begins, the crew sets out to have a successful season. This means ensuring the priorities are clear and that every crewmember stays focused on the priorities as they practice day to day and week to week in preparation for each coming race. That's how improvements are made and races are won. It takes having everyone in the boat rowing the same direction.

This is not dissimilar to what you strive to accomplish in the business world. You want to have a successful performance year where your people know where the team or organization is headed and are actively engaged in helping get there. But let's take a look at what's happening in reality:

According to millions of Gallup poll* participants:

- Only 29 percent of employees are engaged at work
- 54 percent are not engaged in their job
- 17 percent are actively disengaged

*Vital Friends by Tom Rath

If these statistics hit a little too close to home, you may wonder what you can do to get your people actively engaged, realizing their full potential, and collectively contributing to the success of the team or organization.

If you research highly effective organizations, you will find they share a common sense of purpose. Their employees understand where the organization is headed and participate in determining how to get there. These organizations achieve successful outcomes due to a collective effort focused on growing and developing the business. People's contributions are recognized, cementing their dedication and commitment to overall success. With a culture that embraces a common sense of purpose, these organizations successfully navigate their course into the future.

Imagine for a moment...
Everyone in your organization or on your team is in a boat in the middle of the ocean.

You hand them oars and announce, *"Row to our destination!"*

- ***What is happening to your boat?***
- ***What are your people doing?***
- ***What impact does this have on the organization or team?***
- ***The external customer?***

If you find that your boat tends to go around in circles or stall, and people are jumping or being thrown overboard, there may well be a lack of common sense of purpose. It's easy to see that the resulting chaos has a devastating impact on the organization, its performance, and overall success.

Engage your people

Let's take a look at a number of steps you can take to actively engage your people in helping chart and navigate the course into the future. First, provide the answers, or help your people find the answers to the following three questions.

1. What is this organization all about?

Communicating where your organization needs to be and what it stands for and believes in, is critical whether you have a formal Vision, Mission, and Values or not. The answer to this question builds employee, customer, and vendor understanding and sets the tone for getting everyone in the boat rowing the same direction.

2. Where is the organization going, and how will it get there?

Communicating clear direction begins to answer this second question. Your people need to know what the critical-few organizational priorities are and goals to focus on. In addition, when you share the outcomes that need to be accomplished throughout the performance year, your people can begin seeing how what they do fits into the overall picture.

3. How and where do I fit?

Employees need to have a line-of-sight to understand how what they do contributes to overall success. They need to understand their role and know what decision authority they have. When they have answers to the first two questions, departments and teams can develop and implement plans and actions that support attainment of organizational goals. Providing the answer to "How and where do I fit?" focuses individuals on the responsibilities of their jobs and promotes working together for the greater good.

As mentioned earlier, strong organizational cultures have a commonality of purpose that permeates the organization. Employees have a clear understanding of the fundamental reason for the organization's existance and where it is heading. Shared decision-making uses the Values, Vision, and Mission as the basis for decisions. In these strong cultures, employees understand how what they do contributes to the overall success. They strive to make a difference and enjoy being part of a winning organization.

Examine your organization's sense of purpose

Take a few minutes to complete the following self-assessment.

First, decide which group you will assess. The organization? A department? A team? Now, keep this group *top of mind*, as you proceed through the self-assessment. Your ratings will identify conditions that contribute to a well-defined and understood common purpose and pinpoint areas that need additional focus and attention.

The Self-Assessment includes ten pairs of statements representing factors that contribute to establishing and maintaining a common sense of purpose. Read the statement in the left-hand and right-hand column for each contributing factor. Place an "x" on the scale of one to seven that indicates where you view the team, department, or organization *today* in relationship to the two statements. If you find that part of the description rates higher and part lower, plot the lower rating on the scale of one to seven.

Here is an example of one pair of statements, and the rating scale:

CONTRIBUTING FACTOR:	WHERE WE ARE	WHERE WE NEED TO BE
Common Purpose: Direction, priorities, and roles are unclear; focus is on short-term action with little regard for long-term impacts.	x 1 2 3 4 5 6 7	**Common Purpose:** Strategic direction, clear priorities, and associated roles and responsibilities are developed and well understood.

If you decided to have other people participate in the self-assessment process, keep this in mind: People generally believe that their team or organization falls into a high-performing category. However, when I have facilitated the self-assessment process, I've noticed that, as groups review the summary of their individual ratings, they are astonished to find they've rated themselves extremely low. They even suggest that they must have been thinking about the organization when they applied the rating—certainly not their team.

When this situation became a barrier to moving forward with plans and actions to improve the team's effectiveness, I had them retake the self-assessment, being sure to focus on their team or group. In every situation, the overall ratings came out the same or lower than the original assessment.

The moral of the story:

- Ensure that everyone participating in the self-assessment is clear about which group he or she is assessing.

- Assure everyone that the overall assessment simply provides a starting point for developing plans and implementing actions that will increase the team or group's effectiveness.

If participants tell you, "It's tough settling on a rating," it's likely they feel that the group does well against some parts of the description and not so well against others. As a result, they have a tough time assigning a rating. Share the following example, which will help them feel more comfortable applying a rating.

> *As you read the statements in the left-hand and right hand columns, let's say you believe that priorities are pretty well defined and communicated throughout the organization (a 6 rating), but a formal Strategic Plan does not exist (a 3 rating). Confusion about roles and responsibilities, and who makes which decisions surfaces regularly (a 2 rating). Though the organization does a good job of addressing the day-to-day operations, you would like to see a better balance between short-term and long-term focus and action (a 3 rating). You just came up with one 2, two 3s, and one 6 rating.*

> *As you select an overall rating for this Contributing Factor, "err on the low side" to ensure that areas receiving 2 and 3 ratings get addressed. In this example, you may choose to give Common Purpose an overall rating of 2.5.*

Now, take a few minutes to complete the "power10" self- assessment on the following page for your organization or team.

Common Purpose Assessment for: _____

(i.e. ABC Company, Sales Department, Financial Team)

Read the statements in the left-hand and right-hand columns for each of the ten Contributing Factors. Place an "x" on the scale of one to seven that indicates where you view the team, department, or organization today in relationship to the two statements.

CONTRIBUTING FACTOR:	WHERE WE ARE	WHERE WE NEED TO BE
Common Purpose: Direction, priorities, and roles are unclear; focus is on short-term action with little regard for long-term impacts.	1 2 3 4 5 6 7	**Common Purpose:** Strategic direction, clear priorities, and associated roles and responsibilities are developed and well understood.
Alignment: Members work in functional silos with little understanding of their impact on overall success.	1 2 3 4 5 6 7	**Alignment:** Members have a clear understanding of how what they do contributes to overall success.
Mission: The group's purpose is not clearly defined or regularly communicated.	1 2 3 4 5 6 7	**Mission:** The group's over-riding purpose is well defined and regularly used to guide decisions and actions.
Priorities: There are multiple priorities, resulting in confusion and a lack of consistent focus.	1 2 3 4 5 6 7	**Priorities:** Clear priorities are established, communicated, and well understood.
Goals and Objectives: Goals and objectives are not clearly defined or reinforced.	1 2 3 4 5 6 7	**Goals and Objectives:** There are established goals and objectives that members actively focus on achieving.
Plans and Actions: Plans and actions are not developed or aligned to achieve overriding goals and objectives.	1 2 3 4 5 6 7	**Plans and Actions:** Comprehensive plans and actions are in place to support attainment of common goals.
Roles and Responsibilities: Roles and responsibilities are unclear, causing confusion and a lack of accountability.	1 2 3 4 5 6 7	**Roles and Responsibilities:** There are well defined roles and responsibilities, and a clear understanding of where accountability lies.
Measures: There is a lack of defined measures to understand progress and gauge success.	1 2 3 4 5 6 7	**Measures:** Measures are applied and regularly utilized to monitor progress and gauge success.
Performance Reviews: There is not a systematic or consistent approach to reviewing or improving performance	1 2 3 4 5 6 7	**Performance Reviews:** Regular performance reviews are conducted to celebrate successes and identify areas for continued focus and improvement.
Reward and Recognition: There is not a defined plan or consistent approach to rewarding and recognizing performance contributions.	1 2 3 4 5 6 7	**Reward and Recognition:** Reward and recognition are consistently utilized to reinforce performance that supports attainment of short-term and long-term goals.

Where does your organization or team need to focus?

To pinpoint which factors need the most work to strengthen a common sense of purpose, review your assessment and enter the three highest-rated and lowest-rated contributing factors below.

Which three Contributing Factors did you rate the highest? (closest to seven)	Which three Contributing Factors did you rate the lowest? (closest to one)
1.	1.
2.	2.
3.	3.

Next Steps

- For those contributing factors rated the highest, keep doing what you are doing.
- For those contributing factors rated the lowest, establish and take action to address them.

Note: If you completed the assessment on your own and found value in this exercise, consider expanding the self-assessment to include other members of the organization or team. For example:

1. Have the Executive Team complete the self-assessment on the organization.
2. Compile and summarize their ratings on a single, blank assessment sheet.
3. Utilize the assessment summary as the basis for discussion.
4. Clarify which areas require plans and actions to affect improvement.
5. Delegate responsibility for developing plans and actions to existing teams or standing committees.
6. You may also choose to commission a task force to take charge of the planning process for a specific set of contributing factors.

Expanding involvement provides additional insights, commitment, and support, which contributes to the common purpose of the organization.

If you have multiple teams or departments that you would like to participate in the self-assessment process, contact us at www.businesspaths.net to learn more about our on-line assessment services.

Do you need to set clear direction?

I remember being contacted by a newly appointed President who wanted to establish a Strategic Plan for his organization. When I asked if the organization had a current Strategic Plan, he responded, "Yes, I have a drop file in my desk six inches thick labeled Strategic Plan." All I could say was, "Oh my, Michael. If you have to weigh it, it will never be managed." He was delighted to find that a Strategic Plan could fit on one sheet of paper. Granted, the tactical plans and actions will fill additional pages, but Strategic direction can be shared externally and internally using a tri-fold brochure and/or a couple of pages on a web site.

If overall direction and priorities need work, you will find the following information helpful in getting everyone in the boat rowing the same direction.

Take Action—Call for a "power10"!

Why have a Strategic Plan?

Setting clear direction is a vital Leadership role. The development and implementation of a concise Strategic Plan sets clear direction and provides the foundation necessary to establish a common sense of purpose. Organizational strategy clarifies what the organization stands for and believes in, identifies where it's going, and establishes a framework for how it plans to get there.

Though no universal model exists, a Strategic Plan generally consists of six components:

1. Values
2. Vision
3. Mission

} Establish a foundation of understanding

4. Strategic Initiatives
5. Goals
6. Objectives

} Set clear direction and priorities

Here's how a three-to-five-year plan can play out:

Strategic Plan Component	Year 1	Year 2	Year 3	Year 4	Year 5
Values					
Vision	Developed well, the Values, Vision and Mission become reasonably timeless				
Mission					
Strategic Plan Component	**Year 1**	**Year 2**	**Year 3**	**Year 4**	**Year 5**
Strategic Initiatives	Initially developed for 3-5 years	Review in advance of each performance year and update if major external or internal conditions change			
Goals	Initially established for 3-5 years	Review in advance of each performance year and update if needed			
Objectives	Establish outcomes needed for year 1	Update for year 2	Update for year 3	Update for year 4	Update for year 5

Over the years, I have worked with organizations where leadership has a good grasp of the strategy but hasn't committed it to paper. Documenting your strategy provides the opportunity to review, test, modify, and easily share the strategic direction and priorities of the organization. If you find yourself in this position, I strongly encourage you to take time to document your plan. If you find that there are missing components, round out your current plan.

If your organization has no Strategic Plan, I would strongly recommend enlisting outside resources to facilitate the group-planning process. This will ensure that you can actively participate in the planning, rather than trying to participate, facilitate discussion, and develop the plan.

Let's take a look at the overall planning process. The following flow chart displays the components of strategic and tactical planning. It points out that strategy focuses on the 'whats,' and tactics focus on the 'hows' that will deliver the 'whats.' Be sure to keep this distinction in mind as you enter strategic planning.

Establishing metrics provides a means for gauging progress and success along the way to achieving the Mission and Vision. And the proper organizational structure and systems provide support mechanisms that make it easier to achieve the strategic intent.

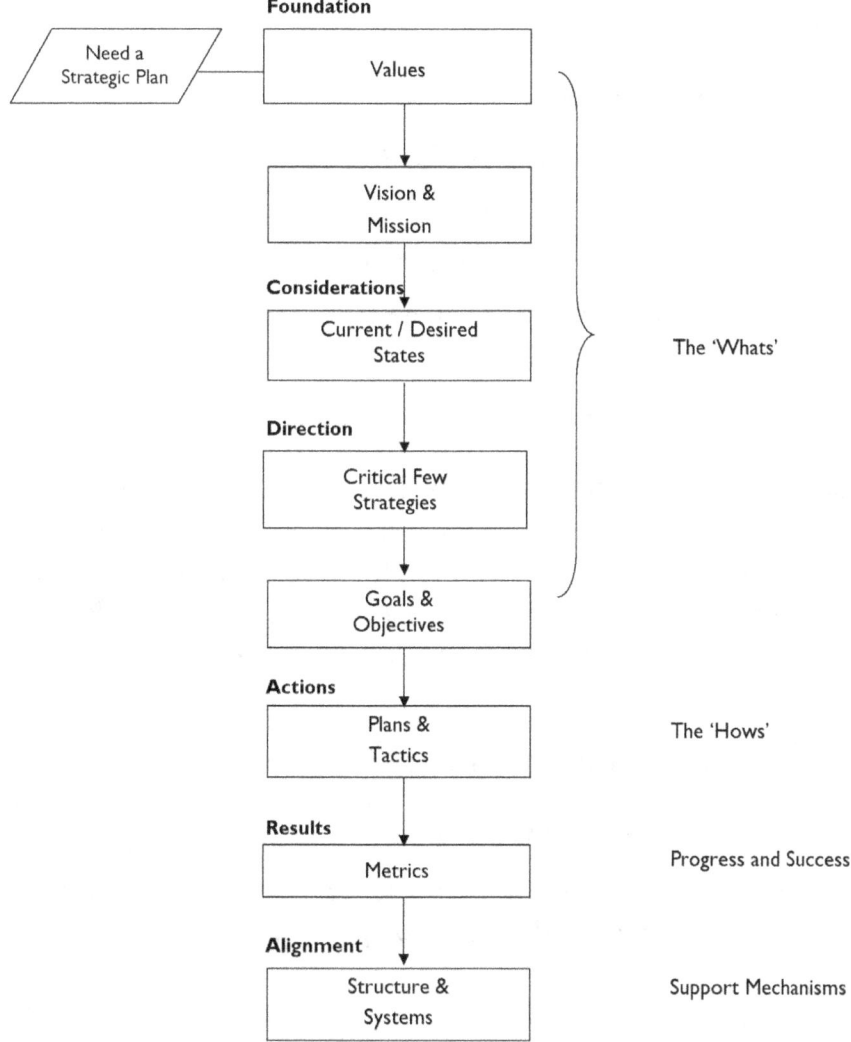

Did You Know?

- 90% of Strategic Plans do not get executed effectively
- Typically <5% of employees know what the strategy is

How can you possibly get everyone in the boat rowing the same direction if they have no idea where the organization or team is heading or how it will get there?

To ensure that everyone hears the same message, once the strategy is developed, it needs to be communicated throughout the organization. This begins building a common understanding of the organization's direction and priorities.

Next, departments and/or teams should set their goals to get everyone in the boat rowing in the same direction. The development of their plans and actions should support team and organizational achievement. For example:

What team and/or department plans and actions are needed to:

- Deliver quality products and services?
- Build customer loyalty and advocacy?
- Ensure the right people are in the right jobs?
- Develop and utilize effective processes and systems?
- Contribute to the financial objectives?

Note: All plans should include a means for measuring progress and success (metrics).

Though the planning process begins at the organizational level, it needs to cascade down through the organization to the individual level to build commonality of purpose. With goals, plans, actions, and metrics established at the department and team level, the next step in building a common purpose involves setting individual expectations. They should include what the employee needs to contribute to the achievement of team and organizational goals and objectives.

A closer look at strategic planning...

The foundation: Values, Vision, and Mission

The Values, Vision, and Mission establish a foundation of understanding on which the initiatives, goals, and objectives are built. Here are the three components with their purpose and benefit:

	Purpose:	Benefit:
Values	Values describe how you want people to act, consistent with attainment of the Vision and Mission.	Values shape the culture and clarify the behaviors that contribute to organizational success.
Vision	A Vision paints a compelling picture of the future you wish to create. It describes what the organization is striving to achieve. Visions inspire people to rally behind the effort and willingly take part in the journey.	A Vision describes how the organization would like to be viewed and what it wants to be remembered for. It creates a "pull" rather than having the past "push," which results in greater forward movement.
Mission	A Mission defines the unique purpose, or the fundamental reason, for the organization's existence.	A Mission provides a consistent basis for decisions and actions and acts as a tie-breaker.

Direction: Strategic Initiatives, Goals, and Objectives

The second half of the strategic plan sets direction with Strategic Initiatives and their respective goals and objectives. Each component and respective purpose and benefit is listed below.

Set clear direction:

	Purpose:	Benefit:
Strategic Initiatives	Strategic Initiatives reflect critical success factors that need focus and action to close the "gap" between where the organization is currently and where it needs to be in the future.	Strategic Initiatives define three to five year priorities for the organization
Goals	Goals reflect the end toward which effort will be directed over the next three to five years	Goals with their associated metrics provide a means of measuring progress and success against attainment of the Vision.
Objectives	Objectives define outcomes that need to be realized over the next 12 to 18 months to move toward achievement of the three- to five-year goals.	Objectives are milestones that allow organizations to gauge progress against attainment of the three to five-year Goals.

Goals and objectives for each Strategic Initiative should meet the "S.M.A.R.T." test which means that they are:

Specific   Goals and objectives should be specific enough that you know when they have been achieved. *Example:* "Being the best we can be" is far too vague.

Measurable   Ensure that you have a way to measure the achievement of goals and objectives.

Achievable   Goals should cause the organization to stretch to achieve them. Objectives should reflect needed outcomes that are realistic in terms of process capability, resource, and time.

Relevant   Goals and objectives should focus on the achievement of the strategic intent.

Time-based   If you use the above parameters, goals and objectives will be time based: three to five years for goals, 12 to 18 months for objectives.

When you consider that 90 percent of Strategic Plans do not get executed effectively, many are too big to effectively implement with available resources. Focus on the critical few success factors, critical few goals, and critical few objectives to end up with a manageable Strategic Plan. When you apply the 20/80 rule, it suggests that 20 percent of the focus and action will provide 80 percent of the payback.

Once you have a Strategic Plan:

1. Each of the people assigned responsibility for ensuring delivery of the objectives needs to bring the proper people together for tactical planning and implementation.

2. The President/CEO needs to plan and schedule a method for communicating the Strategic Plan to all employees. In order to get everyone in the boat rowing the same direction, they must know what the organization stands for and believes in, where it is going, and how it is going to get there. By providing a line of sight, people can understand how what they do contributes to the overall success of the organization.

3. Departments and teams need to establish their goals and develop and implement plans and actions based on the roles they play in the organization. Plans and Tactics define specific actions that will be taken to achieve the 12 to 18 month Objectives and begin closing the gap between where the organization is and where it needs to be three to five years from now.

4. All plans and actions need to include how they will gauge progress and success.

5. The President/CEO needs to schedule regular sessions and bring the responsible parties together to provide a status and report on the progress and success of their group's plans and actions.

NOTE: Understanding the strategic direction is critical for planning at the department, team, and individual level. However, even in the absence of a Strategic Plan at the organizational level, your people can still be "in the boat" rowing the same direction. If you want everyone in the department or on the team in the boat rowing the same direction, lead the effort to develop and implement a plan at the department or team level so that—across the team or throughout the department—there is understanding and a solid foundation of common purpose.

Common Purpose	
Insights	**Tips**
• A Strategic Plan provides a consistent basis for setting clear direction. • Cross-functional involvement in planning expands ownership and commitment. • Implementation and monitoring is critical to success. • By getting everyone in the boat rowing the same direction, the organization will arrive at its destination.	• Enlist outside resources to facilitate the Strategic Planning process. • Include a cross-section of people in planning. • Focus on the critical few vs. the insignificant many priorities. • Share organizational priorities with all employees. • Have departments and teams develop and implement tactical plans and actions that support overall organizational success. • Monitor progress on a regular basis. • Celebrate successes!

Performance Management

Get your organization or team performing consistently well

In rowing, the Coxswain sets expectations with her crew, observes performance during practice, and provides needed coaching to ensure that her team is poised to compete in the coming race. Similarly your responsibility, whether your organization provides products or services, is to ensure that your team or organization performs consistently well and delivers the desired results.

During my years in consulting, I have worked with organizations that appear to be successful on the surface. But they have gotten there due to luck and as a matter of circumstance. Their leaders often live in fear of facing unexpected storms that will capsize their organizational boat and leave the business and employees in jeopardy.

In addition, in a Sirota Survey Intelligence Study over a 3-year period, 3.5 million staff members say:

- Their managers actually hamper progress vs. driving the business
- Staff members have three basic desires:
  1) To know what is expected of them
  2) Have competent bosses
  3) Have better cooperation across the organization
- The biggest challenge for companies is creating an enthusiastic work force

What sets highly successful organizations apart?

Highly successful organizations know what their customers want, and they consistently deliver quality products and relevant services that meet their customers' needs. A commonality of purpose permeates the organization. And, in addition, they have a sound Performance Management Process that supports the delivery of consistent and sustainable results.

You will also find that teams and individuals know how what they do fits into the overall picture. With their understanding of the strategies, goals, and objectives, they know what they need to do to contribute to the success of the organization.

Key indicators and metrics are in place to ensure that everyone knows how they're doing on an ongoing basis. And they guide decisions for knowing where to apply focus and take action.

Having a sound Performance Management Process makes the difference between delivering mediocre, good, or outstanding performance

Put your labor dollars to work

In today's and tomorrow's environment, organizations will be hard pressed to deliver strong, consistent performance if they fail to have everyone actively engaged in striving for organizational success. As I shared in the chapter on Common Purpose:

According to millions of Gallup poll* participants:

- Only 29 percent of employees are engaged at work
- 54 percent are not engaged in their jobs
- 17 percent are actively disengaged

*Vital Friends by Tom Rath

Wow, with that level of disengagement, how strong can performance be? And imagine what level of performance could be achieved if everyone was in the boat rowing the same direction!

Labor costs represent the single largest expense organizations have. So, one question I regularly ask my clients is:

"When you hand out paychecks every month, how do you know you are getting the return on your labor dollar investment that you need?"

A "deer in the headlights" look speaks volumes about the culture and the effectiveness of the organization, as it charts its course into the future. How can the organization reach its full potential without engaging everyone in delivering consistent performance? How will they know what progress is being made? How can leaders develop their people to be the best they can be without establishing goals, setting expectations, and holding their people accountable for delivering them?

Start with engaging your people

Let's take a look at what you can do to get your people engaged. In the chapter on *Common Purpose* there were three questions you needed to provide or help your people find the answers to:

1. What is this organization all about?
2. Where is it going and how is it going to get there?
3. How and where do I fit?

The answers to these questions lay the foundation for getting your people actively engaged in delivering organizational success. With a clear view of where the organization is going, they need answers to the following questions to understand their roles and responsibilities:

1. What is expected of me?

People want to do a good job. First, they need to learn what the organization is all about and where it is headed. Then they need to sit down with their manager to understand what's expected of them and how their performance will be evaluated on an ongoing basis. The combination allows them to see how their contributions support both team and organizational success.

2. How can I make a difference?

People want to be part of a winning organization. In addition to sharing expectations, you need to encourage your people to look for new and innovative ways to continuously improve how the work is done and performance is achieved. When you tap into your people's knowledge and creativity, the result is engaged people who challenge themselves to contribute even more.

3. How am I doing?

Employees need to know that you value them and will recognize them for their contributions. Providing regular coaching and feedback is essential to people performing consistently well. They need to know how they are performing against expectations, or if course corrections are needed. When you develop your people to be the best they can be, you will have an engaged workforce that delivers consistent results.

How effective is your Performance Management Process?

Take a few minutes to complete the following self-assessment.

First, decide which group you will assess. The organization? A department? A team? Now, keep this group "top of mind," as you proceed through the self-assessment. Your ratings will identify conditions that contribute to a sound Performance Management Process, and pinpoint areas that need additional focus and attention.

The Self-Assessment includes ten pairs of statements that represent contributing factors to establishing and maintaining a Performance Management Process. Read the statement in the left-hand and right-hand column for each contributing factor. Place an "x" on the scale of one to seven that indicates where you view the team, department, or organization *today* in relationship to the two statements. If you find that part of the description rates higher and part lower, plot the lower rating on the scale of one to seven.

Here is an example of one pair of statements and the rating scale:

CONTRIBUTING FACTOR:	WHERE WE ARE	WHERE WE NEED TO BE
Performance Management: There are inconsistencies in how performance is reviewed or little understanding of where focus and improvement are needed.	X 1 2 3 4 5 6 7	**Performance Management:** Performance is reviewed on a regular basis to celebrate accomplishments and identify areas requiring continued focus and improvement.

If you decide to have other people participate in the self-assessment process, keep this in mind: People generally believe that their team or organization falls into a high-performing category. However, when I have facilitated the self-assessment process, I've noticed as groups review the summary of their individual ratings, they are astonished to find that they've rated themselves extremely low. They even suggest that they must have been thinking about the organization when they applied the rating—certainly not their team.

When this situation became a barrier to moving forward with plans and actions to improve the team's effectiveness, I had them retake the self-assessment, being sure to focus on their team or group. In every situation, the overall ratings came out the same or lower than the original assessment.

The moral of the story:

- Ensure that everyone participating in the self-assessment is clear about which group he or she is assessing.
- Assure them that the overall assessment simply provides a starting point for developing plans and implementing actions that will increase the team or group's effectiveness.

If participants tell you, "It's tough settling on a rating," it's likely they feel that the group does well against some parts of the description and not so well against others. As a result, they have a tough time assigning a rating. Share the following example, which will help them feel more comfortable applying a rating.

As you read the statements in the left-hand and right-hand columns, let's say you believe that performance is reviewed on occasion (a 4 rating), but there is little to no celebration of accomplishments (a 2 rating). Areas needing focus and improvement get sporadic attention (a 1 rating). You just came up with one 4, one 2, and one 1 rating.

As you select an overall rating for this Contributing Factor, "err on the low side" to ensure that areas receiving 1 and 2 ratings get addressed. In the example, you may choose to give Performance Management an overall rating of 2.5.

Now, take a few minutes to complete the "power10" self-assessment on the following page for your organization or team.

Performance Management Assessment for: _____

(i.e. ABC Company, Sales Department, Financial Team)

Read the statements in the left-hand and right-hand columns for each of the ten Contributing Factors. Place an "x" on the scale of one to seven that indicates where you view the team, department, or organization *today* in relationship to the two statements.

CONTRIBUTING FACTOR	WHERE WE ARE	WHERE WE NEED TO BE
Performance Management: There are inconsistencies in how performance is reviewed or little understanding of where focus and improvement are needed.	1 2 3 4 5 6 7	**Performance Management:** Performance is reviewed on a regular basis to celebrate accomplishments and identify areas requiring continued focus and improvement.
Management Information: Performance indicators are not well defined or produced on a regular basis.	1 2 3 4 5 6 7	**Management Information:** A comprehensive information system exists that reflects current performance trends and results.
Common Goals: Goals are not well defined, communicated, or well understood	1 2 3 4 5 6 7	**Common Goals:** Goals are clear, and members understand how their contributions support attainment of the common goals.
Expectations: Expectations are unclear or not aligned with the overall direction.	1 2 3 4 5 6 7	**Expectations:** There is a clear set of performance expectations, with associated measures that are aligned with the overall direction.
Training and Development: There is little understanding of the knowledge and skills required to support current and future needs.	1 2 3 4 5 6 7	**Training and Development:** Training and personal development plans are established to addresses current and future needs.
Coaching: There is an absence of coaching and feedback to enhance knowledge and improve skills and performance.	1 2 3 4 5 6 7	**Coaching:** Ongoing coaching and feedback are provided to enhance knowledge and develop skills to improve performance.
Informal Feedback: There is a lack of systematic performance monitoring and feedback.	1 2 3 4 5 6 7	**Informal Feedback:** Performance is monitored throughout the review period, and feedback is provided to support improvement opportunities.
Formal Feedback: There is not a formal or consistent process for assessing individual or team performance.	1 2 3 4 5 6 7	**Formal Feedback:** Annual performance appraisals are conducted to recognize contributions and communicate areas needing continued focus or corrective action.
Accountability: There is a lack of consistency in holding members accountable for delivering performance results.	1 2 3 4 5 6 7	**Accountability:** Members are held accountable for delivering desired performance results.
Reward and Recognition: There is not an effective plan in place to reward ongoing contributions and achievements	1 2 3 4 5 6 7	**Reward and Recognition:** Formal and informal recognition plans are established to provide reward and recognition for achieving the desired results.

Where does your organization or team need to focus?

To pinpoint which factors need work to shore up your performance management process, review your assessment and enter the three highest-rated and lowest-rated factors below.

Which three Contributing Factors did you rate the highest? (closest to seven)	Which three Contributing Factors did you rate the lowest? (closest to one)
1.	
2.	
3.	

Next Steps

- For those contributing factors rated the highest, keep doing what you are doing.
- For those contributing factors rated the lowest, take action to address them.

Note: If you completed the self-assessment on your own and found value in the exercise, consider expanding the self-assessment to include other members of the organization or team. For example:

1. Have the Executive Team complete the self-assessment on the organization.
2. Compile and summarize their ratings on a single, blank assessment sheet.
3. Utilize the assessment summary as the basis for discussion.
4. Delegate responsibility for developing plans and actions to existing teams or standing committees.
5. You may also choose to commission a task force to take charge of the planning process for a specific set of contributing factors.

Expanding involvement provides additional insights, commitment and support for the organization's performance management process.

If you have multiple teams or departments that you would like to participate in the self-assessment process, contact us at www.businesspaths.net to learn more about our on-line assessment services.

Are your performance expectations high enough?

Whether your organization provides products or services, you are responsible for working through your people to deliver the desired levels of performance. How effectively you motivate and engage your people in working together and running the day-to-day business determines the level of success the team or organization will achieve.

As a leader, you play either an enabling or a limiting role in your organization or team's performance. How you view performance deliverables becomes critical to success. If you believe the organization or team cannot achieve a given level of performance, they won't, because you will serve as a self-limiter. If you believe the organization or team can accomplish great things, they will, because you will function as an enabler to their success. This is very important to remember, as you work to develop or strengthen your Performance Management Process.

Take Action—Call for a "power10"!

Start the year out right

Each performance year brings a new set of goals that need to be achieved. How you convey the new goals to your people will set the stage for the year's performance. The "planned" level of performance should represent the *minimum level* of acceptable performance your team or organization will deliver.

All too often, teams work toward achieving the planned level of performance by year's end, only to fall short of performance expectations. Successful organizations develop actions to overachieve annual goals before the end of the year arrives.

It is important that you work from the premise that the planned level of performance is the minimum performance required. Then work with your people to develop plans and actions to achieve and over-achieve the planned level of performance for the year.

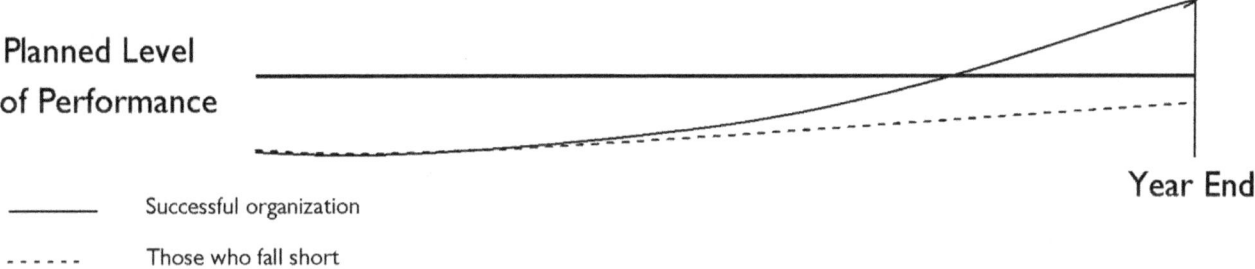

Planned Level
of Performance

Year End

———— Successful organization

- - - - - - Those who fall short

Set department and team goals

As discussed in the chapter on *Common Purpose*, strategic direction provides a foundation upon which the departments and teams build their plans and actions. It clarifies what the organization stands for and believes in, identifies where it's going, and establishes a framework for how it plans to get there.

For most organizations, the basic building blocks for success include:

- Meeting customer requirements
- Providing quality products and services
- Having the right people in the right jobs
- Utilizing effective systems and processes to deliver the business
- Achieving financial objectives

Once developed, strategy should be communicated throughout the organization. This allows everyone to "get in the boat," because they have a common understanding of the organization's direction and priorities.

To get everyone "rowing in the same direction," departments and teams need to set annual goals based on their role in the organization. For example, does the team or department have an impact on delivering quality products and services? Building customer loyalty? Ensuring that the right people are in the right jobs? Developing and continuously improving processes and systems for how the work is done? Contributing to the financial objectives?

As I have worked with organizations large and small, when I asked, "What constitutes success?" answers I've been given ranged from, "If we make payroll, we're in good shape," to "Our metrics show that employees do a great job satisfying our customers. As a result, we're experiencing growth and exceeding profit objectives."

Setting goals begins with understanding what constitutes success for your organization or team. With the organization's priorities in mind, list the areas your team or department will impact on the following table:

Organization's Priority:	Department/Team Impact:	Goal:
Example: Build Customer Loyalty	• Response Time • Solve problems in a timely manner	• Return customer calls within one hour • Resolve or agree on resolution within eight business hours • No customer call-backs for unresolved problems
Customer Satisfaction and Loyalty		
Product/Service Quality		
Financial Performance		
Process and Systems Effectiveness		
Employee Motivation and Satisfaction		
Other _____		
Other _____		
Other _____		

All goals should meet the S.M.A.R.T. test: Specific, Measurable, Achievable, Relevant, Time-based

Establish metrics

Now it's time to decide what metrics you will use to measure performance.

Establishing metrics provides a means for gauging progress and success, and they play a significant role in performance management. In spite of their importance, establishing metrics provides a significant challenge for most organizations and teams.

If you can't measure it, you can't control it. If you can't control it, you can't manage it. If you can't manage it, does it really exist?

What are metrics?

Metrics provide the basis for gauging progress and success throughout the organization. They provide a means for understanding:

- How effectively the organization's strategy is carried out and how strategic goals and objectives are achieved
- How consistently customer needs are being met
- How effectively available resources are being utilized
- How the achievement of functional, team, and individual goals is progressing

Why are metrics important?

What gets measured becomes important!

Metrics are important because they:

- Provide performance and trend data
- Provide data for fact-based decision-making
- Allow you to quantify progress and success
- Help people understand the priorities
- Place focus on efforts that count the most
- Provide insight into how well processes are working
- Become the basis for continuous improvement
- Provide objective information for performance evaluation

- Help you communicate direction, establish accountability, track performance, allocate resources, pursue improvements

If you establish goals or expectations that have no way to be measured, the message you send is that the given performance area is simply not that important. With no method for gauging progress and success, you do not have a consistent way to recognize people for their contributions. When you allow progress and results to be determined based on perception vs. fact, your boat may arrive at its intended destination, but it will most likely have arrived there by pure chance.

Leading and lagging indicators:

There are two types of indicators—leading and lagging. Leading indicators allow you to gauge progress toward achievement of a goal, much like the first downs made in pursuit of a touchdown. In this example, the leading indicators are the first downs. The lagging indicator is the touchdown.

Here's a business example: Let's say you decide to use the "Overall Satisfaction Rating" on your customer survey as the key indicator for measuring Customer Satisfaction and Loyalty (a lagging indicator). However, in your service business, other indicators such as response time and equipment uptime (both leading indicators) historically have a strong influence on the overall satisfaction of your customers. By tracking response time and equipment uptime, you can anticipate the possibility of an upcoming shift in the Overall Customer Satisfaction rating. Leading indicators allow you to take preventive actions to positively impact performance eventually expressed by the lagging indicator.

Apply the S.M.A.R.T. test

As mentioned above, goals need to meet the S.M.A.R.T. Test. Let's use Building Customer Loyalty as an example of how to apply it.

Let's say that you identified responding to customer needs and solving customer problems in a timely manner as key activities that the department and/or team need to do to build customer loyalty.

To develop goals that are specific and measurable for these two activities, you should ask yourself:

- How quickly do our customers expect to receive a return phone call?
- How long do our customers expect to wait for their problem to be resolved?
- If we are unable to solve a customer problem immediately, what is a reasonable amount of time to research the problem, identify potential solutions, and get back in touch with the customer to negotiate a final resolution?
- What can we reasonably deliver on a consistent basis?

If customer input is not available to answer these questions, put on your "customer hat" and explore what *your* expectations would be from an organization that is similar to yours.

Organization's Priority:	Department/Team Impact:	Goal:
Example: Build Customer Loyalty	• Respond to customer needs • Solve customer problems in a timely manner	• Return customer calls within one hour • Resolve or agree on resolution within eight business hours • No customer call-backs for unresolved problems

In this example, the decision was made to:

- Return calls within one hour
- Resolve customer problems within eight business hours, or
- Conduct research, identify potential solutions, and get back to the customer to negotiate resolution within eight business hours
- There should be no customer call-backs for unresolved problems

Are your new goals ready to be implemented?

- What information do you currently have available to measure your performance in these areas?
- What do you need to put in place to effectively measure the identified performance elements?

Once you have settled on your key indicators/metrics, I strongly recommend that you develop a Monthly Performance Trend Report to review on a regular basis. It will provide a snapshot of performance and allow you to ask pertinent questions to understand conditions that drive the trends positively and negatively. With a trend report in place, you can always ask for additional drill-down information to support needed planning or problem-solving efforts. You will find trend report examples on pages 75 and 76.

With the Department/Team goals established and metrics applied, you have a solid foundation for communicating, monitoring, and sharing performance with your people on a regular basis.

In today's fast-paced, competitive environment, no organization can afford to leave its success and future to chance.

Build in accountability

Having a Performance Management Process provides the basis for accountability throughout the organization.

Over the past several decades, many organizations have found themselves in an "era of entitlement," versus one of accountability. There has been an absence of clear direction and expectations, and they lack a sound method for gauging their progress and success. Many have moved away from conducting Performance Reviews. As a result, they find themselves reacting to daily challenges instead of focused on key deliverables that drive their success. In addition, there is an absence of reward and recognition for individual and group contributions.

How do you motivate your people and get them actively engaged in finding new and innovative ways to do the work and deliver performance? How do you ensure they feel valued for their contributions if there is no way to gauge progress and success? How do you hold people accountable for contributing to the success of the organization?

Without accountability: Entitlement reigns. Turnover adds to instability. People are not engaged in their work. Good employees leave because poor performance has not been addressed. People do not feel valued. There is little opportunity for professional growth. The organization's most valuable asset becomes disenfranchised. Performance suffers.

Set and manage individual expectations

With department and team goals established, it's time to set expectations with each of your people.

In a Sirota Survey Intelligence Study of 34,300 employees:

- 33 percent of management thought their organizations were doing enough to deal with poor performance
- 43 percent of non-management thought their organizations were doing enough to deal with poor performance

---

When two thirds of managers and over half of the employees think their organization is not doing enough to deal with poor performance, something has got to change.

Employees want to be part of a winning organization. In order for them to contribute to the overall success, they need to know what is expected of them and how what they do makes a difference. They need to have a clear understanding of their roles and responsibilities, to include decision authority. They need coaching and feedback throughout the year to reinforce those things they are doing well and point out areas that need improvement.

How to implement an Individual Performance Planning and Evaluation process

In the chapter, "Your Leadership Role," I pointed out that your primary internal customers are the people who report directly to you. Your role is to develop them to be the best they can be, because it is through your people that the team, department, and organization will be successful.

Having a sound Performance Planning and Evaluation process is key to developing your people. It allows your employees to 1) know what is expected of them, 2) develop and implement a personal action plan to meet those expectations, and 3) receive the coaching and feedback they need to perform successfully.

Let's assume that everyone wants to do a good job. Though you may argue an individual case or two, generally this is true. If you want everyone to do his or her best and work together toward common goals, it is important to ensure that there is a consistent approach for establishing performance standards, providing feedback, and evaluating employees' performance against expectations.

Over the past twenty years, I have asked many managers, "If there was one thing you could eliminate from your management role that would make your job easier, what would it be?" Almost to the person, the response is to eliminate performance appraisals.

Well, many organizations have done precisely that. Some never put the process in place to begin with. They see writing and administering performance reviews as a cumbersome and time-consuming process. Unfortunately, they fail to understand the significant value that can be realized when they invest their time developing their most valuable asset...their people.

As I've worked with managers to develop their people, a common concern regularly surfaced: They dislike performing activities that might generate conflict. The fear of conflict is magnified when the ongoing activities that make writing and administrating Performance Evaluations a positive learning and growth experience are not happening in a consistent and timely manner. Consequently, managers found themselves needing to write and administer performance reviews without having done a good job of establishing expectations and/or providing regular coaching and feedback. As a result, employees were given reviews that were better than their performance warranted, or they were surprised by concerns that had not previously been communicated.

The Performance Cycle

Let's take a look at a typical performance cycle that begins when an employee is hired and review tools that support each step in the process. The last six steps are repeated every year of an employee's employment.

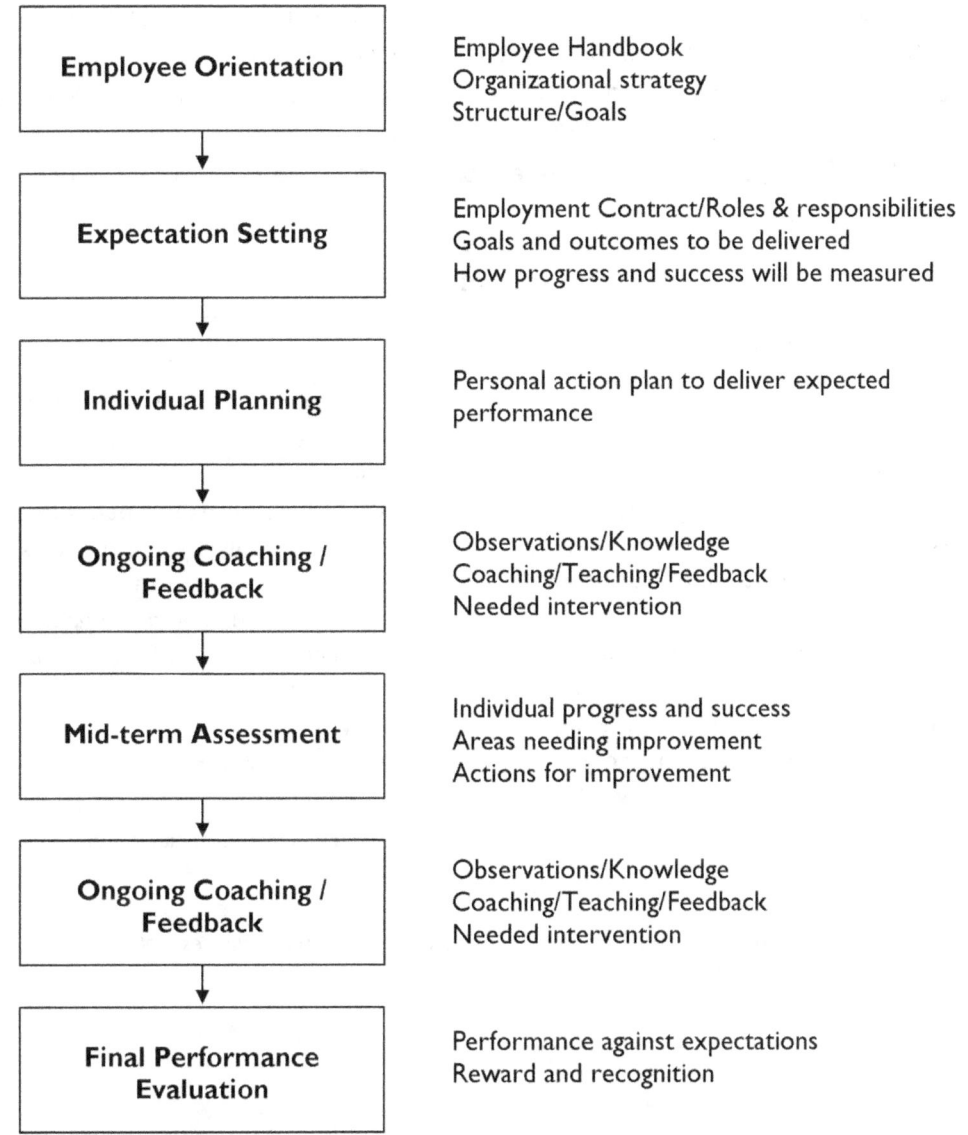

Employee Orientation	Employee Handbook Organizational strategy Structure/Goals
Expectation Setting	Employment Contract/Roles & responsibilities Goals and outcomes to be delivered How progress and success will be measured
Individual Planning	Personal action plan to deliver expected performance
Ongoing Coaching / Feedback	Observations/Knowledge Coaching/Teaching/Feedback Needed intervention
Mid-term Assessment	Individual progress and success Areas needing improvement Actions for improvement
Ongoing Coaching / Feedback	Observations/Knowledge Coaching/Teaching/Feedback Needed intervention
Final Performance Evaluation	Performance against expectations Reward and recognition

Make sure it happens

To ensure that you make Performance Planning and Evaluation a meaningful and productive process, you need to schedule the required activities on your calendar at the beginning of the year —when you will set expectations, time for inspection, coaching and feedback, when you will conduct interim and final evaluations. Then, should a scheduling conflict arise, you can make a conscious decision to move the Performance Planning and Evaluation activity to another date and time during the same month.

What I've found is that, if you fail to schedule the required activities as the year begins, daily challenges nip at your heels and end up taking priority. As a result, you can find yourself down to the wire needing to write and administer Performance Evaluations, without having completed the activities necessary to make it a meaningful and rewarding process.

There is nothing worse than allowing time to get away from you, have the year fly by, and all of a sudden November rolls around. You find yourself in a position where you need to write all your people's performance evaluations without having spent any time with them throughout the year. Your strong performers have not received the recognition they deserve, and your poor performers have not had the benefit of your coaching and feedback to improve their performance.

Performance Management	
Insights	**Tips**
<ul><li>People are your most valuable asset.</li><li>They want to be part of a winning organization.</li><li>A sound Performance Management Process can make the difference between delivering mediocre, good, or outstanding performance.</li><li>You can be a self-limiter or an enabler to performance.</li><li>Goals need to meet the S.M.A.R.T. test.</li><li>The people who report to you are your primary internal customers.</li></ul>	<ul><li>Labor is your single largest expense.</li><li>Make sure your expectations are high enough.</li><li>What gets measured becomes important.</li><li>Use a monthly trend report to provide snapshots of performance.</li><li>Schedule your full-year performance-management activities at the beginning of the year.</li><li>Stay on schedule.</li><li>Hold people accountable.</li><li>Don't leave your success to chance.</li><li>Address sub-standard performance.</li></ul>

For information about available products and services visit www.businesspaths.net

Key Indicator Trend Report - EXAMPLE **ABC Company**

Key Indicators:	Planned Performance:	Jan	Feb	Mar	Apr	May	Jun	JuneYTD
FINANCIAL PERFORMANCE								
Net Profit	Annually 20%	($1.0)	($0.4)	$2.7	$5.2	$7.6	$8.2	$22.3
Revenue	$25K monthly average	$18.7	$19.1	$22.5	$25.0	$27.6	$29.5	$23.7
Expense	$20K monthly average	$19.7	$19.5	$19.8	$19.8	$20.0	$21.3	$20.0
Market Share								
New Business	5 customers per month	0	1	2	4	6	7	20
Current Customer Growth	15% revenue increase	0	2%	2%	6%	5%	12.5%	6.70%
Customer Cancellations	0	0	0	0	1	0	0	1
CUSTOMER LOYALTY								
Overall Satisfaction	95% Satisfied or Very	96.1%	95.0%	95.0%	87.3%	92.5%	94.2%	93.7%
Customer Complaints	0	0	0	2	0	1	0	3
Overall Responsiveness	98% Very satisfied	95.00%	97.20%	100.0%	98.10%	96.0%	95.4%	96.3%
Return calls	98% <2 hours	100%	98%	95%	99%	98%	97%	98%
Problem resolution	95% Within 1 week	98%	95%	100%	95%	93%	100%	96%
PRODUCT/SERVICE QUALITY								
Product Reliability	95% up-time	91%	87%	94%	96%	81%	95%	86%
Call Backs / Returns	0	5	8	0	12	0	3	28
Service Relevance	95% Satisfied or Very	87%	93%	99%	91%	95%	97%	93%
Repeat Business	15% incremental revenue	8%	10%	17%	12%	15%	16%	14%
EMPLOYEE MOTIVATION								
Overall Satisfaction	95% Satisfied or Very	92%						
Turnover	<5%	20%	0	0	0	0	0	20%
Productivity								
Revenue per Employee	$5K monthly average	$3.7K	$3.8K	$4.5K	$5.0K	$5.5K	$5.9K	$4.7K
Absence	< 5 hours monthly average	0	0	8	16	0	0	24

Key Indicator Trend Report

ABC Company

Key Indicators:	Planned Performance:	June YTD	Jul	Aug	Sept	Oct	Nov	Dec	YTD
FINANCIAL PERFORMANCE									
Net Profit	Annually 20%								
Revenue	$25K monthly average								
Expense	$20K monthly average								
Market Share									
New Business	5 customers per month								
Current Customer Growth	15% revenue increase								
Customer Cancellations	0								
CUSTOMER LOYALTY									
Overall Satisfaction	95% Satisfied or Very								
Customer Complaints	0								
Overall Responsiveness	98% Very satisfied								
Return calls	98% <2 hours								
Problem resolution	95% Within I week								
PRODUCT/SERVICE QUALITY									
Product Reliability	95% up-time								
Call Backs / Returns	0								
Service Relevance	95% Satisfied or Very								
Repeat Business	15% incremental revenue								
EMPLOYEE MOTIVATION									
Overall Satisfaction	95% Satisfied or Very								
Turnover	<5%								
Productivity									
Revenue per Employee	$5K monthly average								
Absence	< 5 hours monthly average								

Delegation and Empowerment

Get your people actively involved

Economic tightening has organizations scrambling to do more with less. Our constantly changing environment drives the need for increased flexibility and agility to ensure responsiveness to both customer and business demands. With the complexity of today's business, organizations need everyone in the boat actively rowing in the same direction.

In the world of rowing crewmembers are invested in doing their best. They make requests for certain drills and to do things differently to improve their approach and win the race. This is similar to business, where delegation and empowerment are essential to effectively leading an organization and achieving a competitive advantage.

How will you ensure that your people are actively engaged and contributing to overall success?

Only 45 percent of respondents say they are satisfied with their jobs, down from 61.1 percent in 1987, the first year the survey was conducted

TNS survey of 5000 U.S. Households

"Challenging and meaningful work is vitally important to engaging American workers."

John Gibbons, Program Director of Employee Engagement Research

"The downward trend in job satisfaction could spell trouble for the overall engagement of U.S. employees and ultimately employee productivity."

Lynn Franco, Director of the Consumer Research Center

The Conference Board Press Release Jan. 5, 2010

"power10" Leadership embraces the belief that people are an organization's most valuable asset, and the primary role of all managers and leaders is to develop their people to be the best they can be. It is through your people that you and the organization will succeed. Consequently, when only 45 percent of people express satisfaction with their jobs, I have to ask, "Why?" and "What will it take to get people engaged and increase their satisfaction?"

While visiting organizations over the years, I could usually sense the health of the work environment, as I entered the office. In fact, in some cases, my initial instinct was to turn around and walk right back out the door. How effectively these organizations functioned and their level of success aligned with my initial perception. They were filled with unhappy people, their turnover was high, and performance was less than desirable. Those initial perceptions spoke volumes.

In contrast, I visited many organizations that felt warm and welcoming upon entering. People were smiling and upbeat, openly sharing information about their organization. They experienced limited turnover and successfully achieved their performance objectives. Wow! What a difference!

When people feel valued, are actively engaged in their work, and feel they can make a difference, they enjoy getting up and coming to work. And, if you're asking yourself how you can increase your people's involvement and satisfaction, read on.

Delegate and empower your people

What constitutes delegation and empowerment? These terms are basically synonymous, though some may argue that *delegation* does not carry with it the decision authority that empowerment does. You will find that the term *empowerment* is used most frequently in today's environment.

When you give a person or group of persons the authority to act on your behalf, that is delegation and empowerment. When you give them responsibility for a specific task or performance area, including decision authority, and you hold them accountable for the output and/or outcomes, you are delegating and empowering your people. Providing boundaries is part of the process, but ultimately the final output and/or outcome is the responsibility of the empowered person(s). When leaders empower their people they are giving up control in lieu of trust.

Avoid the pitfalls

With organizational flattening, decision-making and problem-solving have shifted closer to the customer. Empowering your most valuable asset, your people, to respond to changing customer requirements and address ongoing business needs is critical to your success both today and in the future. You need everyone actively engaged in running the day-to-day business, looking for new and innovative ways to improve how the work is done and how performance is achieved.

This does not mean, however, that delegation and empowerment come without their own set of challenges.

Since empowerment came into vogue, there have been many failed attempts to effectively implement it. All too often attempts resembled abdication of responsibility, rather than true empowerment. Managers and leaders "dumped" responsibilities on their people without clarifying:

1) What needed to be accomplished

2) What decision authority their people had

3) What time-frames were required, and

4) The boundaries they needed to work within

Little consideration was given to whether their people had the requisite knowledge and skills to take on these new challenges. Many managers simply walked away and waited for the performance to be delivered, or "the magic to happen." When it didn't, or the approach was not to the manager's liking, they would chastise their people for not embracing their new-found empowerment, take back responsibility, and walk away thinking, "This empowerment stuff doesn't work." And, as a result, the lack of management guidance and support left their people feeling exploited and abandoned.

Imagine a situation where you serve on a task force and give it your all, only to have your work rejected by the person who commissioned the task force in the first place. Maybe they are uncomfortable with the approach your task force took. Or they don't care for the recommendation or outcome that was presented. Regardless of how things got to this point, members of the task force most likely feel that they wasted their time and energy. And they feel exploited, used, and unappreciated— definitely not interested in volunteering for another task force any time soon.

When people take responsibility for a new activity, or serve on a task force, they need to know if they have decision authority or if they are only allowed to make recommendations.

In an environment where people are told "what to do" and "how to do it," responsibility and accountability reside with the manager. Conversely, in an empowered environment, leaders share what needs to be accomplished, engage their people in determining "how" to accomplish it, and hold them accountable for outcomes.

How successful a role empowerment plays in an organization depends on several factors:

Organizational Culture

- Does the organization's leadership have a tolerance for risk?

- Will they be supportive of employees when mistakes are made?

- Are they capable of providing a high level of autonomy to their people?

Workforce Competence

- Do the employees have the ability to work autonomously?

- Has their business approach proven to be trustworthy?

- Are they motivated to assume additional responsibility?

As you review these questions, allow your answers to guide your approach, as you extend empowerment to your people.

Reap the rewards

Organizations committed to the successful implementation of empowerment reap many rewards. You will find that they enjoy both individual and organizational growth. Management time is freed up, because employees take responsibility for solving problems, making decisions, and improving how the work is done and performance is achieved. Decision-making improves, employee satisfaction and commitment increases, and manager-employee relationships grow stronger.

If you want to reap similar rewards, you need to willingly relinquish control, tap into your people's knowledge and creativity, and trust that your people will do the right thing given the chance. This does not mean that your involvement diminishes. You need to set boundaries, train and coach your people, oversee the process, intervene when needed, and hold your people accountable.

Is delegation and empowerment alive and well in your organization?

Take a few minutes to complete the following self-assessment.

First, decide which group you will assess. The organization? A department? A team? Now, keep this group "top of mind," as you proceed through the self-assessment. Your ratings will identify conditions that contribute to increased delegation and empowerment and pinpoint areas that need additional focus and attention.

The Self-Assessment includes ten pairs of statements that represent contributing factors to increasing delegation and empowerment. Read the statement in the left-hand and right-hand column for each contributing factor. Place an "x" on the scale of one to seven that indicates where you view the team, department, or organization *today* in relationship to the two statements. If you find that part of the description rates higher and part lower, plot the lower rating on the scale of one to seven.

Here is an example of one pair of statements and the rating scale:

CONTRIBUTING FACTOR:	WHERE WE ARE	WHERE WE NEED TO BE
Delegation and Empowerment: Decisions are made at management levels and shared with members for implementation.	x 1 2 3 4 5 6 7	**Delegation and Empowerment:** Members are actively involved in making decisions that affect their work and take full responsibility and accountability for the outcomes.

As mentioned previously, if you decide to have other people participate in the self-assessment process, keep this in mind: People generally believe that their team or organization falls into a high-performing category. However, when I have facilitated the self-assessment process, I've noticed that, as groups review the summary of their individual ratings, they are astonished to find that they've rated themselves extremely low. They even suggest that they must have been thinking about the organization when they applied the rating—certainly not their team.

When this situation became a barrier to moving forward with plans and actions to improve the team's effectiveness, I had them retake the self-assessment, being sure to focus on their team or group. In every situation, the overall ratings came out the same or lower than the original assessment.

The moral of the story:

- Ensure that everyone participating in the self-assessment is clear about which group he or she will assess.
- Assure them that the overall assessment simply provides a starting point for plan-development and action-implementation that will increase the team or group's effectiveness.

If participants tell you, "It's tough settling on a rating," it's likely they feel that the group does well against some parts of the description and not so well against others. As a result, they have a tough time assigning a rating. Offer the following example, which will help them feel more comfortable applying a rating.

> *As you read the statements in the left-hand and right-hand columns, let's say you believe that overall management makes most of the decisions (a 2 rating), but those decisions are generally shared with team members (a 6 rating). Only select members of the team are asked for their input (a 1 rating), and there is little ownership for the result of decisions (a 2 rating). You just came up with two 2s, one 6, and one 1 rating.*

> *As you select an overall rating for this Contributing Factor, "err on the low side" to ensure that areas receiving 1 and 2 ratings get addressed. In the example, you may choose to give Delegation and Empowerment an overall rating of 2.5.*

***Now, take a few minutes to complete the "power10" self-assessment
on the following page for your organization or team.***

*Delegation and Empowerment Assessment for:*_____

(i.e. ABC Company, Sales Department, Financial Team)

Read the statements in the left-hand and right-hand columns for each of the ten Contributing Factors. Place an "x" on the scale of one to seven that indicates where you view the team, department, or organization *today* in relationship to the two statements.

CONTRIBUTING FACTOR	WHERE WE ARE	WHERE WE NEED TO BE
Delegation and Empowerment: Decisions are made at management levels and shared with members for implementation.	1 2 3 4 5 6 7	**Delegation and Empowerment:** Members are actively involved in making decisions that affect their work and take full responsibility and accountability for the outcomes.
Authority: Members are reluctant to make decisions; most are deferred to management.	1 2 3 4 5 6 7	**Authority:** Members have a clear understanding of the decisions they are empowered to make.
Boundaries: Boundaries are not well defined, causing mistrust of management and confusion surrounding direction and priorities.	1 2 3 4 5 6 7	**Boundaries:** Managers define and communicate appropriate boundaries to guide decisions and actions.
Accountability: Members are reluctant to assume responsibility for their decisions, actions, and performance.	1 2 3 4 5 6 7	**Accountability:** Members are given the authority and responsibility for managing their day-to-day work and are held accountable for delivering desired results.
Control and Influence: Members attempt to resolve issues that are outside their control or influence, resulting in frustration and conflict.	1 2 3 4 5 6 7	**Control and Influence:** Members identify when they have direct control, influence, or no control over the situation and take appropriate action.
Decision Making: Decisions tend to be made in isolation and actions taken without consideration for their consequence.	1 2 3 4 5 6 7	**Decision Making:** Members are skilled at making fact-based decisions that support the attainment of common goals.
Decision Styles: Command decision-making is the predominant style of decision-making applied.	1 2 3 4 5 6 7	**Decision Styles:** There is a good understanding of when command, consultative, collaborative, or consensus decision-making styles should be used.
Inclusion: Members are expected to carry out plans and actions that are established without their input or involvement.	1 2 3 4 5 6 7	**Inclusion:** Members are actively involved in planning and implementing actions that affect their work.
Innovation and Risk Taking: Members are averse to taking risks or making decisions for fear their efforts may fail.	1 2 3 4 5 6 7	**Innovation and Risk Taking**: Members actively seek out and find new and improved ways to approach how the work is done and results are achieved.
Shared Leadership: Members believe it is solely the manager's role to provide needed leadership.	1 2 3 4 5 6 7	**Shared Leadership:** Members partner with the manager to provide leadership.

Where does your organization or team need to focus?

To pinpoint which factors need work to expand delegation and empowerment, review your assessment, and enter the three highest-rated and lowest-rated factors below.

Which three Contributing Factors did you rate the highest? (closest to seven)	Which three Contributing Factors did you rate the lowest? (closest to one)
1.	
2.	
3.	

Next Steps

- For those contributing factors rated the highest, keep doing what you are doing.
- For those contributing factors rated the lowest, take action to address them.

If you completed the self-assessment on your own and found value in the exercise, consider expanding the self-assessment to include other members of the organization or team. For example:

1. Have the Executive Team complete the self-assessment on the organization.
2. Compile and summarize their ratings on a single, blank assessment sheet.
3. Utilize the assessment summary as the basis for discussion.
4. Delegate responsibility for developing plans and actions to existing teams or standing committees.
5. You may also choose to commission a task force to take charge of the planning process for a specific set of contributing factors.

Expanding involvement provides additional insights, commitment, and support for delegation and empowerment throughout the organization.

If you have multiple teams or departments that you would like to participate in the self-assessment process, contact us at www.businesspaths.net to learn more about our on-line assessment services.

Find opportunities for empowerment

When you empower your people, they become partners in the business versus cogs in the wheel. Empowerment provides them with continuous learning opportunities and involves them in adapting to an ever-changing environment. If empowerment is new to your team or organization, your people will need to learn to take initiative, be creative, and accept responsibility for their actions.

Take a few minutes to list operational activities and tasks that are performed on a regular basis, noting who currently performs them. Circle those that you currently perform, which your people could be doing.

Daily activity/task	Who	Weekly activity/task	Who	Monthly activity/task	Who
Example: activity reporting	workers	Team meeting	me	Example: work schedule	me

If you are just beginning to introduce empowerment to your team or organization, decide which two or three activities will be the priority. I recommend that you begin with a few priorities, rather than addressing all identified activities/tasks at one time. Also, decide whom you will empower to handle these tasks.

Clarify your boundaries

Boundaries provide a framework for the people you are empowering to work within. They generally clarify decision authority, time requirements, resource impacts, and financial parameters for the project or activity.

For example: You decide that your team leaders should work with their team members to set their work schedule. The boundaries you set for your team leaders might include the following:

- The work schedule needs to maximize productivity (resource impact)
- Protect responsiveness to customers (potential financial impact)
- Minimize the need for overtime (resource impact)
- One person on vacation at a time (decision authority)
- The schedule needs to be complete, with a copy to you by the 25th of each month (time requirement)

When you meet with your team leaders to empower them, address any questions they have, and determine what training they need to successfully take on this new responsibility.

For those empowerment opportunities you plan to act on, enter them below, indicate whom you will empower, list your boundaries, and enter any training required to support the shift in responsibility. Decide when you will transition each activity and when you will incorporate this in your action plan.

Activity/task	Who I am empowering	My boundaries	Training needed
Example:			
Team work schedules	Team leaders	- The work schedule needs to maximize productivity - Protect responsiveness to customers - Minimize the need for overtime - Limit the number of people on vacation at one time - The schedule needs to be complete, with a copy to you by the 25th of each month	- Challenges that regularly arise - How to use the scheduling system

As your team leaders assume their new responsibilities, schedule frequent meetings with them. Inform them of your expectation that they come prepared to report how things are going, share concerns they have, and ask for any guidance they need. Your time together will also provide you the opportunity to intervene should it be necessary. You will find fewer meetings are needed as they become more comfortable with the process for setting work schedules.

Take Action—Call for a "power10"!

Transfer decision-making authority

An important step in delegation and empowerment is the transfer of decision-making authority. Decision-making styles and team roles change as you involve and empower your people to take increased responsibility and accountability for running the day-to-day business. When they feel trusted to make decisions that affect their jobs, work becomes more meaningful to them.

As you empower your people, clarify who makes what decisions, and ensure that they know what style of decision-making to use in various situations. Let's take a look at the four forms of decision-making.

Decision style:

Command   Made by an individual when time constraints do not allow for input or when time is of the essence

Example: A manager is made aware that another team is in dire need of temporary resources. They make a decision on the spot to lend three people to the effort for up to one week, and then inform their people of the decision.

Consultative   When the person(s) responsible for a decision asks for and considers input or recommendations before they make the final decision

Example: A manager who is planning a quarterly meeting asks the team for topics of interest and gives them consideration as the agenda is built.

Collaborative   Made when a group that has shared responsibility works together to make a collective decision

Example: Managers find themselves overwhelmed with a new program launch. They work together to address the problem and decide how to ensure consistent implementation.

Consensus   When a group with common goals, listens to and understands each member's point of view and reaches a decision that all support. Though it may not be an individual's first choice, they will support it because it was reached in an open and fair manner.

Example: Team leaders are empowered to develop a meaningful recognition plan for their teams. Through the process, they gather input, hear everyone's ideas and rationale, and reach a consensus decision on the final plan.

Clarify roles and responsibilities

As mentioned at the beginning of this chapter, the advent of participative leadership came with confusion surrounding the true meaning of empowerment (i.e., giving someone the responsibility, as well as the decision-making authority for a task).

One of the challenges that surfaced had people believing that consensus was the only form of decision-making. They believed that, if they were empowered, everyone had to agree on the decision, and whatever decisions they made should stand. If their manager failed to support the decisions, they saw the manager as giving lip service vs. true empowerment. To avoid this problem and support successful empowerment, communicate your boundaries and be clear about who has what decision-making authority.

Empowerment affects both you and your people's roles and responsibilities. And, in order for people to do a good job, they need to know what's expected of them and what decisions they are empowered to make.

A consistent challenge I often see organizations face is ensuring that their employees have clearly defined roles and responsibilities. In the absence of role clarity, confusion and chaos abound. The following parable reminds us of the importance of clarifying people's roles and responsibilities.

Everybody, Somebody, Anybody, and Nobody

Once upon a time, there were four people:

Their names were Everybody, Somebody, Anybody and Nobody.

Whenever there was an important job to be done, Everybody was sure that Somebody would do it.

Anybody could have done it, but Nobody did it.

When Nobody did it, Everybody got angry because it was Everybody's job.

Everybody thought that Somebody would do it, but Nobody realized that Nobody would do it.

So, consequently, Everybody blamed Somebody when Nobody did what Anybody could have done in the first place.

If your organization has documented roles and responsibilities, ensure that they get updated, as your people take on additional responsibilities and decision-making authority. If roles and responsibilities are not currently documented, I recommend taking the time to do so. As I mentioned earlier, role clarity is a significant challenge for most organizations. By clarifying roles and responsibilities you will minimize the opportunity for confusion and chaos.

Lead more, manage less

Your role changes when you introduce empowerment to your team or organization. You will need to lead more and manage less, which brings change to the current culture.

If you work in a command and control environment where people are told what to do and how to do it, managers are likely to expect implementation and compliance from their people. Consequently, you will generally find:

- A focus on doing things right
- A dependence on management
- One-way, top-down communication
- Imposed change
- A focus on individual contributions

- Centralized decision-making
- Limited empowerment

The shift to participative leadership and empowerment paves the way for *sharing where the organization needs to be* and *engaging members of the organization to help determine how to get there*. In this environment you need to focus on:

- Doing the right things
- Development at all levels of the organization
- Innovation and risk taking
- A team and process focus
- Negotiation and collaboration
- Empowerment and accountability
- Shared visions and team strategies
- Continuous improvement

The transition from command and control to participation and empowerment, finds managers expanding their leadership role. They invest their time being a change agent, communicator, coach, facilitator, and a boundary manager.

As you lead your people, you will unleash their creativity, tap into their knowledge and experience, and empower them to run the day-to-day business. They will find your actions enabling, freeing, allowing innovation and risk taking, challenging, flexible, and democratic.

However, this expanded role requires skills that not everyone in management possesses. A manager who has "cut their management teeth" in a command and control environment may be reluctant or unable to adapt to the changing role. Consequently, the way will be paved for a new set of leaders, people ready to set the pace and tone, motivate people, create and develop work teams, and manage a process that consistently delivers performance.

The key lesson to be learned here is that you need to manage things and lead people!

Recapture valuable time

How many hours a week do you work? Would you like to be more effective while investing fewer hours?

Let's start with this reminder:

You are there to ensure that your team or organization effectively handles the volume of work and delivers desired results. How effectively you function in your role will determine how many hours you invest doing your job. When you share responsibility with the people who report to you, more can be accomplished in less time.

First, make sure that your people take full responsibility for all areas of their job. If you have people who regularly come to you looking for solutions, or to have you make decisions that affect their work, there is an opportunity to shift decision-authority to where it belongs.

An article published in the November-December 1974 issue of the *Harvard Business Review*, entitled "Management Time: Who's Got the Monkey," had a huge impact on my management and leadership years, as I learned how to share responsibility. Authors William Oncken, Jr., and Donald L. Bass talk about ensuring that your people's responsibilities do not end up on your desk for action. They use a "monkeys on your back" metaphor to refer to those responsibilities.

In the article, people were not fully embracing their roles and responsibilities. They took problems to their manager seeking solutions. Managers injected themselves into situations their people should handle. The result, managers ended up with so many "monkeys on their backs," they became the bottleneck to getting things done. The wheels of progress slowed…people became frustrated.

One Saturday morning, the manager went into his office to get caught up. As he glanced out his office window, he spotted the people whose "monkeys were on his back." They were across the street teeing off at a local golf course. A light bulb came on, as he quickly assessed the situation. He closed up the office and headed for home to spend the rest of the weekend with his family.

The following Monday morning, the manager met with each of his people to discuss the "monkeys" he had accumulated, and to return them to their rightful owner…the person responsible for each of the monkey's care and feeding.

In the same way, if your team members regularly come to you looking for solutions or to have you make decisions that affect their work, you have an opportunity to shift decision-making authority to where it belongs. Though your people may initially need some guidance and support, you will recapture time as they become more comfortable fulfilling their ongoing responsibilities.

Second, take the activities and tasks you identified earlier in this chapter and begin empowering your people to take on additional responsibility. When you effectively engage your people through delegation, empowerment and role clarity, you will re-capture valuable time.

As you do, make sure you function in your role and ensure that others fully function in theirs. Your people may need some encouragement and training to successfully care for their monkeys. But the investment will be well worth your time.

Third, focus on being more proactive and less reactive. By investing your time in planning and implementation, training and empowerment, you will expand your leadership skills and recapture valuable time.

Whether you have an organization of fifteen, two hundred fifty, or over seven hundred, having everyone in the boat rowing the same direction will allow you to reach the finish line more effectively. Just imagine what can happen when everyone listens to customers, everyone works together to solve problems, and everyone looks for new and innovative ways to run the business and over-achieve performance.

Let's face it; the old ways simply don't work anymore. Lead your people. Develop them to be the best they can be. And empower them to actively participate in running the day-to-day business.

Delegation and Empowerment	
Insights:	**Tips:**
• Your people are your most valuable asset. • Empowerment is critical to success. • Engaged people find their work more meaningful. • Accountability is essential to empowerment. • Empowerment has its challenges. • Training may be needed for new responsibilities. • Roles change as empowerment expands.	• Identify empowerment opportunities. • Make sure people understand what decision authority they have. • Communicate the boundaries you expect people to work within. • Lead more, manage less. • Keep "monkeys" where they belong. • Focus on being proactive vs. reactive.

For information about available products and services visit www.businesspaths.net

Problem Solving

Get everyone solving problems

Problems surface in every organization. Whether you're dealing with performance shortfalls, ineffective work processes, or the need to do more with fewer resources, it is important to effectively address and solve problems. Each problem represents an opportunity to improve how the work is done and results are achieved.

Just as the Coxswain addresses problems solicited from their crew, you can seize opportunities to successfully engage your people in addressing work-related issues. As a result, you and your team will enjoy increased effectiveness, cost savings, and improvements in the quality of products and services.

In your organization or on your team:

- *Who solves the problems that arise?*
- *Do your employees look to you for the solutions?*
- *Are your people active participants in solving problems?*

During my years in leadership roles, one thing became very clear in dealing with problems. People found it much easier to identify problems than to solve them. That needs to change in today and tomorrow's environment…everyone needs to actively participate in identifying and solving ongoing problems.

Focus people's time and energy

With flatter organizations, decision-making and problem-solving have become a shared responsibility. The good news: employees and teams get involved in tackling problems and finding solutions. The bad news: often they are given responsibility without receiving needed training and tools to develop and implement lasting solutions. An inconsistent approach to problem-solving finds people:

- Treating symptoms instead of problems
- Trying to solve problems outside their direct control or influence
- Investing time and energy only to find that the problem recurs.

If you want effective problem-solving efforts, you need to engage the right people to work specific problems. Whether working on an operational issue or working with suppliers or strategic partners, everyone needs to understand what decision authority they have and what boundaries they need to work within. They also need information that supports their ability to make fact-based decisions versus dealing with people's perceptions. When people come together to solve a problem, they will have ownership of, and commitment to, the solutions they select to solve the problem.

Function in your leadership role

How many times has one of your people come to you and said, "Boss, we've got a problem?" It is so easy to allow your people to deposit problems on your desk for resolution. Have you ever ended up with a stack of problems and the progress stopped until you made the next move? If so, you know how it feels to have become a barrier to making progress…not good.

I remember a steady stream of people lining up outside my office to share problems that needed fixing. They seldom came in with any ideas or recommendations on how to solve the problems. Realizing the risk and not wanting to become the barrier to timely solutions, I let them know I would gladly discuss work problems with them if they also brought recommended solutions.

If you find your list of actions growing due to problems your people have deposited on your desk, it's time to take a different approach. Teach your people how to solve problems and empower them to make decisions and take appropriate action. You can always be a resource, but finding solutions should lie with those closest to the problem—your people.

Getting everyone involved in problem solving is new for many organizations and teams. And, if your people are used to being told what to do and how to do it, being asked to make decisions and solve problems can seem scary and feel very risky. It will be important that you help your people understand that you expect them to be actively involved in running the day-to-day business and sharing responsibility for solving problems and delivering performance.

If your team or organization has not been actively involved in solving problems, I strongly recommend that you get everyone trained in problem-solving techniques. This will ensure that you have a common problem-solving language and approach throughout the team and organization.

An important part of your role during this transition involves reinforcing the use of the problem-solving process, providing needed coaching, and removing barriers that get in the way of your people's ability to successfully solve ongoing problems.

How effectively does your organization solve problems?

Take a few minutes to complete the following self-assessment.

First, decide which group you will assess. The organization? A department? A team? Now, keep this group "top of mind," as you proceed through the self-assessment. Your ratings will identify conditions that contribute to effective problem-solving and pinpoint areas that need additional focus and attention.

The Self-Assessment includes ten pairs of statements that represent factors that contribute to establishing and maintaining a sound problem-solving process. Read the statement in the left-hand and right-hand column for each contributing factor. Place an "x" on the scale of one to seven that indicates where you view the team, department, or organization *today* in relationship to the two statements. If you find that part of the description rates higher and part lower, plot the lower rating on the scale of one to seven.

Here is an example of one pair of statements, and the rating scale:

CONTRIBUTING FACTOR:	WHERE WE ARE	WHERE WE NEED TO BE
Problem Solving: Problems are addressed and decisions are made independently or in an unstructured manner.	x 1 2 3 4 5 6 7	**Problem Solving:** Members share responsibility for addressing problems and selecting solutions, utilizing a disciplined, fact-based approach.

If you decided to have other people participate in the self-assessment process, keep this in mind: People generally believe that their team or organization falls into a high-performing category. However, when I have facilitated the self-assessment process, I've noticed that, as groups review the summary of their individual ratings, they are astonished to find they've rated themselves extremely low. They even suggest that they must have been thinking about the organization when they applied the rating—certainly not their team.

When this situation became a barrier to moving forward with plans and actions to improve the team's effectiveness, I had them retake the self-assessment, being sure to focus on their team or group. In every situation, the overall ratings came out the same or lower than the original assessment.

The moral of the story:

- Ensure that everyone participating in the self-assessment is clear about which group he or she is assessing.
- Assure them that the overall assessment simply provides a starting point for developing plans and implementing actions that will increase the team or group's effectiveness.

If participants tell you, "It's tough settling on a rating," it's likely they feel that the group does well against some parts of the description and not so well against others. As a result, they have a tough time assigning a rating. Share the following example, which will help them feel more comfortable applying a rating.

As you read the statements in the left-hand and right-hand columns, let's say you believe that problems are generally addressed (a 6 rating), but decisions are made independently by management (a 2 rating). Members share little responsibility for solving problems (a 1 rating). A disciplined, fact-based approach is not apparent (a 2 rating). You just came up with one 1, two 2s, and one 6 rating.

As you select an overall rating for this Contributing Factor, "err on the low side" to ensure that areas receiving 1 and 2 ratings get addressed. In this example you may choose to give Problem Solving an overall rating of 2.0

Now, take a few minutes to complete the "power10" self-assessment on the following page for your organization or team.

Problem Solving Assessment for:_____

(i.e. ABC Company, Sales Department, Financial Team)

Read the statements in the left-hand and right-hand columns for each of the ten Contributing Factors. Place an "x" on the scale of one to seven that indicates where you view the team, department, or organization *today* in relationship to the two statements.

CONTRIBUTING FACTOR	WHERE WE ARE	WHERE WE NEED TO BE
Problem Solving: Problems are addressed and decisions are made independently or in an unstructured manner.	1 2 3 4 5 6 7	**Problem Solving:** Members share responsibility for addressing problems and selecting solutions, utilizing a disciplined, fact-based approach.
Approach: Problems are approached in an inconsistent manner, which minimizes the overall impact of the efforts.	1 2 3 4 5 6 7	**Approach:** There is a consistent approach to solving problems, which includes the use of common tools and techniques.
Skills: There is no formal training provided to ensure a consistent and effective approach to solving problems.	1 2 3 4 5 6 7	**Skills:** Members receive formal training and regular reinforcement in problem-solving techniques.
Control and Influence: Members invest time and energy attempting to solve problems and address issues that are outside their control or influence.	1 2 3 4 5 6 7	**Control and Influence:** Members address and resolve problems that are inside their control or sphere of influence.
Root Cause: Members often select solutions based on perception versus fact, which results in treating the symptom rather than the root cause.	1 2 3 4 5 6 7	**Root Cause:** Members are effective at gathering critical data and analyzing the problem to understand and address the root cause.
Brainstorming: Plans and actions are developed by a select few and handed off for implementation.	1 2 3 4 5 6 7	**Brainstorming:** Group problem solving is used to generate ideas and build on thoughts that result in sound decisions and effective solutions.
Consensus: There is often hollow commitment to solutions, which results in an inconsistent approach and frustration.	1 2 3 4 5 6 7	**Consensus:** Members recognize the importance of reaching consensus and use it to gain ownership and commitment to solutions.
Benchmarking: Members are reluctant to consider solutions that are "not developed here."	1 2 3 4 5 6 7	**Benchmarking:** Best practices are sought out, researched, and utilized to effect change in a timely and effective manner.
Implementation: There is inconsistent implementation, with limited means of gauging progress and measuring results.	1 2 3 4 5 6 7	**Implementation:** Members are skilled at implementing plans and evaluating the progress and results of selected solutions.
Results: There has not been significant improvement realized through problem-solving efforts.	1 2 3 4 5 6 7	**Results:** Significant benefits have been realized as a result of effective problem-solving efforts.

Where does your organization or team need to focus?

To pinpoint which factors need work to get everyone solving problems, review your assessment and enter the three highest-rated and lowest-rated factors below.

Which three Contributing Factors did you rate the highest? (closest to seven)	Which three Contributing Factors did you rate the lowest? (closest to one)
1.	
2.	
3.	

Next Steps

- For those contributing factors rated the highest, keep doing what you are doing.
- For those contributing factors rated the lowest, take action to address them.

If you completed the self-assessment on your own and found value in the exercise, consider expanding the self-assessment to include other members of the organization or team. For example:

1. Have the Executive Team complete the self-assessment on the Executive Team.
2. Compile and summarize their ratings on a single, blank assessment sheet.
3. Utilize the assessment summary as the basis for discussion.
4. Develop plans and actions.
5. You may also choose to commission a task force to take charge of the planning process for a specific set of contributing factors.

Expanding involvement provides additional insights, commitment, and support, which contributes to the effectiveness of problem solving throughout the organization.

If you have multiple teams or departments that you would like to participate in the self-assessment process, contact us at www.businesspaths.net to learn more about our on-line assessment services.

Treat causes vs. symptoms

If a product fails to meet quality standards, a person fails to follow a prescribed process, or a breakdown occurs in any process or system, there are problems that need to be solved. In order to bring results back into line, action needs to be taken to regain or fix the current approach.

Let's assume that things are rolling along just fine using a standard approach. Then something happens…there is a dip in results. The question becomes, "What happened to cause the 'dip?'" and "What action do we need to take to regain the standard or a better level of performance?" You might picture it as:

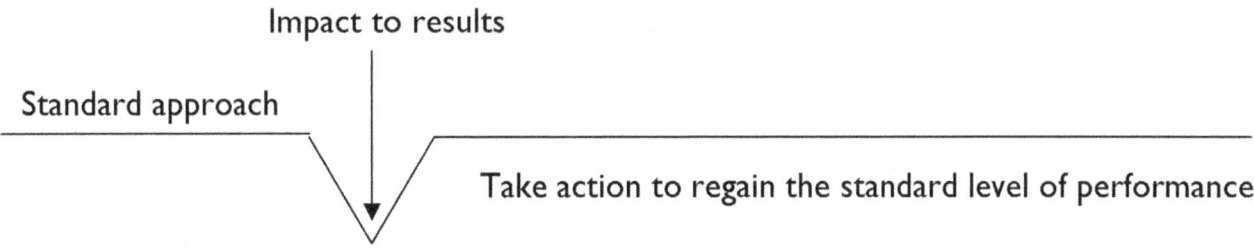

When members of your team or organization deal with problems, are they solved for the long-term, or do they tend to resurface? It is important to ensure that people come together and focus their efforts on finding a lasting solution.

Without a systematic approach to solving problems, you or your people may treat the symptoms, which are only the tip of the iceberg, rather than addressing the root cause. They may also attempt to solve problems that are outside their control or influence, which sets their efforts up to fail.

A key to effective problem solving is to ensure that people don't jump to conclusions about the cause of the problem or how to solve it. It is important to look at the situation and identify the root cause before exploring options and selecting a solution.

Take Action—Call for a "power10"!

Pick a problem you need solved

To introduce you to a standard problem-solving process, select and enter a problem that you need solved on the line below:

Problem: _____

(*Example:* There has been a rash of customer complaints)

Who are the right people to work the problem? Whether you're dealing with a performance shortfall, a product quality issue, or a rash of customer complaints, etc., who should you bring together to solve the problem? Consider who potentially contributes to the problem, if it is isolated to one or multiple areas, which areas might be affected when solved, etc. List them below:

_____   _____

_____   _____

_____   _____

_____   _____

With your problem-solving team identified, it is important that they use a comprehensive problem-solving approach that gets to the root cause of the problem versus treating only the symptoms. That's the only way to enjoy a long-term solution.

Use a standard problem-solving process

There are numerous problem-solving processes out there with varying numbers of steps. Whether they have four or six steps, the general approach is basically the same. You will find a four-step process often combines a couple of steps in the six-step process. My recommendation is the following six-step process.

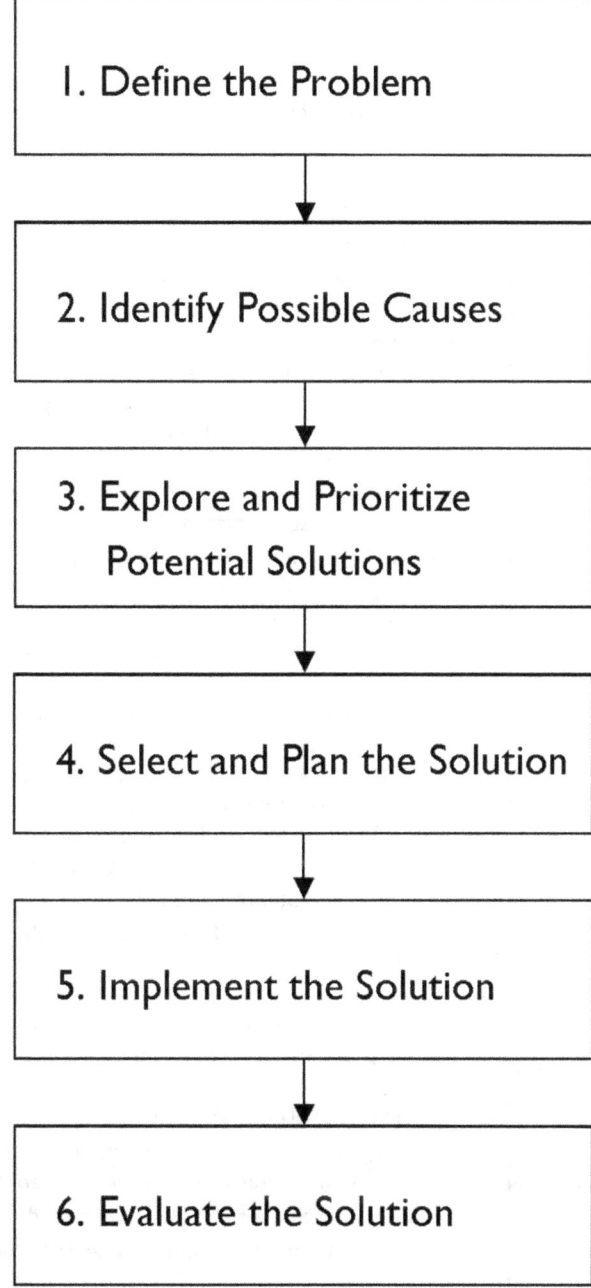

Let's take a closer look at the problem solving steps

With the problem identified and the Problem Solving Team selected, it's time to analyze the problem and select and implement a solution.

There is a two-page Problem Solving Worksheet and example at the end of this chapter for your use. It is designed to guide teams and individuals through the steps of the process, and have them capture their progress along the way.

Here are instructions for the six-step process for your use.

Step 1: Define the Problem	• Describe the current state that exists (where you are today). • If the problem is too general, break it down into smaller parts. • Confirm that the problem is real versus perceived. • Describe the Desired state (where you need to be) in measurable, observable terms. • Enter the current and desired states on the Problem Solving Worksheet and a date you would like to see the problem solved.

Step 2: Identify Possible Causes	• It is important to get to the root cause of the problem.
	• Brainstorm possible causes by asking the group questions like:
	  - Why does this problem exist?
	  - What caused it?
	  - What changed right before the problem surfaced?
	  - Will it resolve itself or just go away?
	• Clarify and combine causes of the problem to reduce the list.
	• Gather and utilize facts to validate the above causes, eliminating those that cannot be substantiated.

Step 3: Explore and Prioritize Potential Solutions	• Review the desired state
	• Using the scrubbed list of possible causes, brainstorm potential solutions by asking questions like:
	  - What will it take to solve the problem?
	  - What solutions have already been thought of?
	  - What new approaches should be considered?
	  - How could we stop this situation from recurring?
	• Prioritize potential solutions.
	• Enter them on the Problem Solving Worksheet found on pages 104 and 105 of this chapter.

Step 4: Select and Plan the Solution	• Review the prioritized list of potential solutions. • Discuss and plan actions that will close the gap between where you are currently and your desired state and enter them on the Problem Solving Worksheet. • Assign responsibility, due dates, and measures for each of the actions and enter them on the Problem Solving Worksheet. • Gain approval for the plan, if required. • Decide what information will be gathered to evaluate each of the actions.
Step 5: Implement the Solution	• Follow the established plan. • Monitor progress against the plan. • Collect data to evaluate the effectiveness of the solution.
Step 6: Evaluate the Solution	• Review progress and collected data on a frequent basis. • If the desired state is achieved, incorporate actions into your Standard Operating Procedures, as required. • Make sure you give the plan ample time to work. • If not achieved, identify new problems and rework actions for implementation, monitoring, and evaluation.

When you or the team evaluates the effectiveness of a solution, you may uncover some new developments that lead to corrections, thus making the solution even more effective. Patience and persistence are important. Unfortunately, I have seen many great plans be abandoned before they have had time to deliver the needed results.

When the solution consistently delivers the desired results, it should be included in your Standard Operating Procedures.

Congratulations! You solved the problem you identified.

Problem Solving	
Insights:	**Tips:**
<ul><li>Problem solving should be a shared responsibility.</li><li>All employees should actively participate in solving problems.</li><li>Using a consistent problem solving approach throughout the organization provides a common language.</li><li>A consistent approach yields the best results.</li></ul>	<ul><li>When you commission a problem-solving team, make sure they know if they are a decision-making body or a recommending body.</li><li>Establish and communicate your boundaries before a problem-solving team begins its work.</li><li>Give solutions ample time to make a difference.</li><li>Share and recognize problem-solving successes.</li></ul>

For information about available products and services visit www.businesspaths.net

Problem Solving Worksheet

1. **Define the problem:**_____
   (The current state that exists)

   Describe the Desired-state: _____
   (In measurable/observable terms)   **Achieve this desired state by:** _____

2. **Identify possible causes:**

   _____

   _____

   _____

   _____

   _____

3. **Explore and prioritize potential solutions**

   _____

   _____

   _____

   _____

Is there additional information required before selecting a solution?   ☐ Yes   ☐ No   **If Yes:**

Information Needed: **Person Responsible:**

_____   _____

_____   _____

Next meeting date: _____

4a. Select and plan the solution:
   Select the solutions that will deliver the desired state. Assign responsibility, establish due dates, and identify how progress and success will be measured.

Prioritized Actions	Responsible Person(s)	Due Date	Measure(s)
1.			
2.			
3.			
4.			

4b. How progress and success will be monitored

For each action, define how and when progress and success will be monitored

Action	How progress and success will be monitored	When it will be monitored
1.		
2.		
3.		
4.		

5. Implement the solution

- Follow the plan
- Monitor progress against the plan
- Collect data to evaluate the effectiveness of the plan

Starting Performance	Progress √	Progress √	Progress √	Progress √
Action 1				
Action 2				
Action 3				
Action 4				

6. Evaluate the solution

Overall			

If the desired state is achieved, incorporate the solutions into your standard operating procedures. If not achieved, identify new conditions and rework actions for implementation, monitoring, and evaluation.

Problem Solving Worksheet – *EXAMPLE*

1. **Define the problem:** Customer complaints tripled over the past month
   (The current state that exists)
   Describe the Desired-state: Reduce complaints to the previous level–an average of two per week
   (In measurable/observable terms)   **Achieve this desired state by:** within 60 days

2. Identify possible causes:

- Customers are unhappy with a newly launched product.

- Half the complaints deal with new product capability.

- Product capability was over sold.

- The product launch was accelerated to respond to competition.

- Sales people were not adequately trained on the new product.

- The product was not ready to go to market.

4. Explore and prioritize potential solutions

- Negotiate solutions with upset customers.

- Check in with all customers who purchased the new product.

- Retrain sales people on new product capability.

- Be explicit about product capability in all advertising and promotion.

- Ensure all employees understand product capability.

Is there additional information required before selecting a solution?   ✓ Yes   ☐ No   If Yes:

Information Needed:
Does advertising and promotion adequately describe product capability?

Person Responsible:
Marketing/Communications Manager

Status: All current advertising and promotion materials are clear about product capability.

                 Next meeting date: Friday at 10:00

4a. Select and plan the solution:

Select the solutions that will deliver the desired state. Assign responsibility, establish due dates, and identify how progress and success will be measured.

Prioritized Actions	Responsible Person(s)	Due Date	Measure(s)
1.A – Negotiate solutions with upset customers.	Sales Reps	by month end	Negotiations complete
2.A – Check in with all customers who purchased the new product.	Sales Reps	Within 60 days	Contact made; satisfaction determined; negotiations complete
3.B – Retrain sales people on new product capability.	Training Manager	Within one week	Training complete
4.B – Ensure all employees understand product capability.	Training Manager	By month end	All employees briefed
5.C – Continue to be explicit about product capability in all future advertising and promotion.	Marketing / Communications Manager	Ongoing	No customer complaints

4b. How progress and success will be monitored

For each action, define how and when progress and success will be monitored

Action	How progress and success will be monitored	When it will be monitored
1.	Negotiations with upset customers	Weekly status meeting Monday at 10:00
2.	Contact with all customers who bought the product	Weekly status meeting Monday at 10:00
3.	Retrain sales reps	Weekly status meeting Monday at 10:00
4.	Brief all employees	Weekly status meeting Monday at 10:00

5. Implement the solution

- Follow the plan
- Monitor progress against the plan
- Collect data to evaluate the effectiveness of the plan

Starting Performance	Progress √	Progress √	Progress √	Progress √
Action 1 – 100 negotiations needed	25 completed	Total of 50 completed	Total of 75 completed	Total of 100 completed
Action 2 – 900 customers to be contacted	125 contacted 20 negotiated	Total of 250 contacted 35 negotiated	Total of 375 contacted 62 negotiated	Total of 500 contacted 80 negotiated; 4 more weeks to monitor
Action 3 – no sales retrained	All but two trained	Two who were on vacation now trained		
Action 4 – no employees briefed	All management and customer service briefed	All service personnel briefed	All administrative personnel briefed	

6. Evaluate the solution

Overall Average of 6 complaints/week	10 complaints this week	7 complaints this week	4 complaints this week	1 complaint this week; 4 more weeks of monitoring

If the desired state is achieved, incorporate the solutions into your standard operating procedures. If not achieved, identify new conditions and rework actions for implementation, monitoring, and evaluation.

Continuous Improvement

Get everyone seeking new and innovative ways

In the world of rowing, there is no moment during a race for the crew to change course. They actively execute the approach they honed during hours of practice in preparation for the coming race.

This is similar to keeping pace with today's business environment, which poses challenges for many organizations. It demands that you embrace change as an integral part of your culture. You need everyone actively engaged in finding new and innovative ways to improve the quality of products and services. And you need your people focused on continuously improving how the work is done and results are achieved.

When you consider that most people do not like change, getting everyone on board presents its own set of challenges. In fact, a 20-50-30 rule reflects people's feelings about change:

- 20 percent welcome the change; they feel it is on target and long overdue.
- 50 percent sit on the fence, unsure whether they should support it or not.
- 30 percent are unhappy with any proposed change, because they prefer things just stay the way they are.

When you look at today's reality, change is inevitable. Increased customer sophistication, global markets, and emerging technologies are but a few of the forces that drive ongoing change. When you add an unstable economy and a workforce that spans six decades, even more factors have an impact on organizations. Those organizations that anticipate and effectively respond to changing conditions master the flexibility and agility they need to maintain a competitive advantage.

With ongoing focus, continuous improvement efforts will eventually transform your team or organization. Innovative products and services, coupled with new and better work processes will improve effectiveness and lead to new business.

Function as a change agent

One of your roles involves that of change agent. In that role, you have responsibility for ensuring that your team or organization becomes more effective at satisfying customers and delivering results.

Maintaining the status quo is not an option when you need to position the organization for future growth and success. A path to success is having:

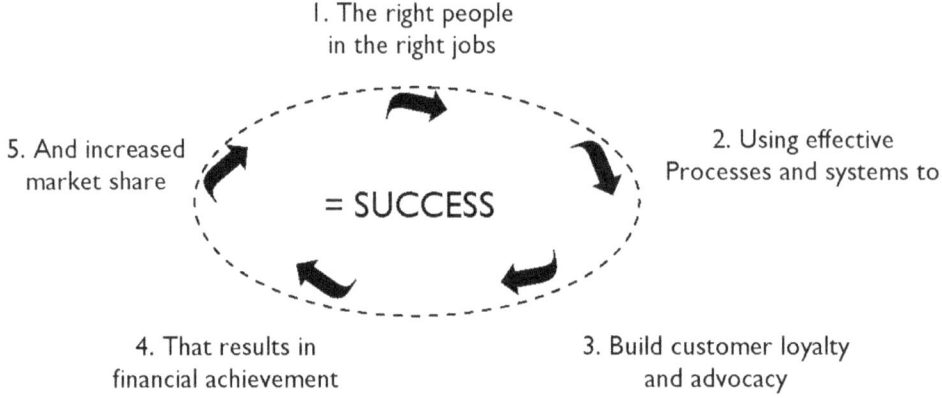

As you look for ways to continuously improve how the work is done and performance is achieved, ask yourself:

- What processes and systems do we have in place today?
- Which ones do we consider the critical few?
- How effectively do these critical few function?
- Which ones need streamlining or a major overhaul?
- What processes do we need to add or eliminate all together?

Your answers will point to opportunities for continuous improvement efforts that make your team or organization more effective.

The sooner change becomes a norm, and continuous improvement a way of life, the easier it becomes to get your people actively involved in making a difference for the team and organization. And, as you tap into their knowledge and expertise, your people will actively seize opportunities for improving how to approach the day-to-day business.

You can tackle even more opportunities when you add the synergy gained from focusing functional, cross-functional, and virtual teams on innovative ways of doing business.

> ***As people come together to find new and innovative ways for improving how the work is done and performance is achieved, they can accomplish great things.***

Continuous improvement or problem solving...that is the question

Let's take a look at the difference between problem solving and continuous improvement.

Problem solving

Problems surface when something alters a standard approach and negatively affects results. When a product fails to meet quality standards, a person fails to follow prescribed procedures, or a breakdown occurs in any process or system problems surface that need resolution. When you apply a systematic problem-solving approach, you can get to the root of the problem. This ensures that corrective action brings the process or procedure back into compliance. As a result, performance gets back on track.

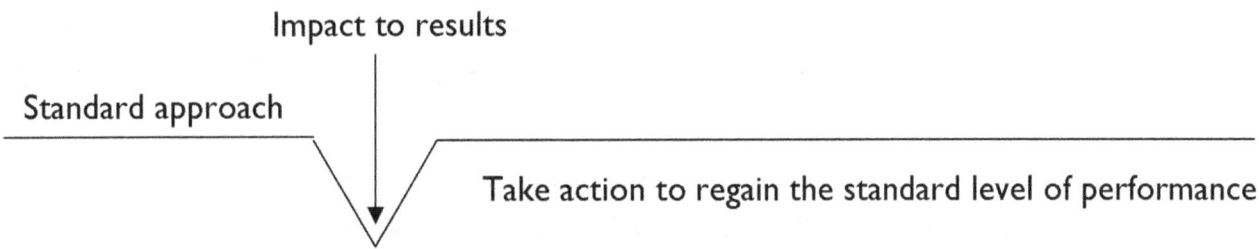

Continuous improvement

Do you need breakthroughs to significantly alter how the work is done? To develop a totally new process? Continuous improvement will support you in those efforts.

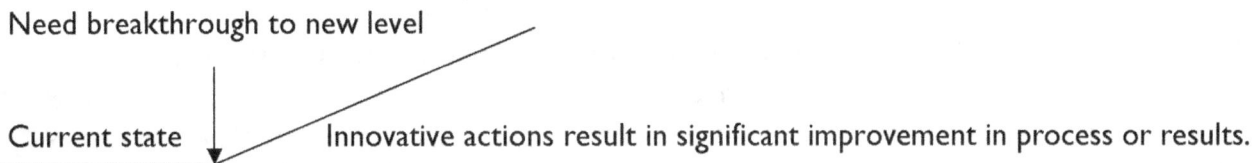

Make continuous improvement a way of life

In light of changing customer and business requirements, continuous improvement needs to become a way of life in your organization.

Whether you choose to use a continuous improvement process, Lean Manufacturing, or Six Sigma, anticipating and responding to changing needs and conditions helps secure and maintain a competitive position in the marketplace. Breakthroughs that move performance to new levels generally result from finding and implementing new and innovative approaches to how work is approached.

Both problem solving and continuous improvement are important processes for all employees to use. With everyone focused on finding and implementing new and innovative ways to improve how the work is done and performance is achieved, your team or organization will become agile and better equipped to respond to changing requirements.

How actively does your team or organization focus on continuous improvement?

Take a few minutes to complete the following self-assessment.

First, decide which group you will assess. The organization? A department? A team? Now, keep this group "top of mind," as you proceed through the self-assessment. Your ratings will identify conditions that contribute to continuous improvement and pinpoint areas that need additional focus and attention.

The Self-Assessment includes ten pairs of statements that represent factors that contribute to a consistent continuous improvement process. Read the statement in the left-hand and right-hand column for each contributing factor. Place an "x" on the scale of one to seven that indicates where you view the team, department, or organization *today* in relationship to the two statements. If you find that part of the description rates higher and part lower, plot the lower rating on the scale of one to seven.

Here is an example of one pair of statements, and the rating scale:

CONTRIBUTING FACTOR:	WHERE WE ARE	WHERE WE NEED TO BE
Continuous Improvement: Multiple priorities leave little time to focus on ways to improve how the work is done.	x 1 2 3 4 5 6 7	**Continuous Improvement:** Members consistently look for new and innovative ways to improve the quality of products and services, and how the work is done.

If you decided to have other people participate in the self-assessment process, keep this in mind: People generally believe that their team or organization falls into a high-performing category. However, when I have facilitated the self-assessment process, I've noticed that, as groups review the summary of their individual ratings, they are astonished to find they've rated themselves extremely low. They even suggest that they must have been thinking about the organization when they applied the rating—certainly not their team.

When this situation became a barrier to moving forward with plans and actions to improve the team's effectiveness, I had them retake the self-assessment, being sure to focus on their team or group. In every situation, the overall ratings came out the same or lower than the original assessment.

The moral of the story:

- Ensure that everyone participating in the self-assessment is clear about which group he or she is assessing.
- Assure them that the overall assessment simply provides a starting point for developing plans and implementing actions that will increase the team or group's effectiveness.

If participants tell you, "It's tough settling on a rating," it's likely they feel that the group does well against some parts of the description and not so well against others. As a result, they have a tough time assigning a rating. Share the following example, which will help them feel more comfortable applying a rating.

> *As you read the statements in the left-hand and right-hand columns, let's say you believe that members find it too risky to offer ideas on how to improve how the work is done (a 1 rating), but the quality of products seems good (a 6 rating). People are not expected to look for ways to improve how the work is done (a 2 rating). You just came up with one 1, one 2, and one 6 rating.*

> *As you select an overall rating for this contributing Factor, "err on the low side" to ensure that areas receiving 1 and 2 ratings get addressed. In this example, you may choose to give Continuous Improvement an overall rating of 2.0*

Now, take a few minutes to complete the "power10" self-assessment on the following page for your organization or team.

Continuous Improvement Assessment for:_____

(i.e. ABC Company, Sales Department, Finance Team)

Read the statements in the left-hand and right-hand columns for each of the ten Contributing Factors. Place an "x" on the scale of one to seven indicating where you view the team, department, or organization *today* in relationship to the two statements.

CONTRIBUTING FACTOR	WHERE WE ARE	WHERE WE NEED TO BE
Continuous Improvement: Multiple priorities leave little time to focus on ways to improve how the work is done.	1 2 3 4 5 6 7	**Continuous Improvement**: Members consistently look for new and innovative ways to improve the quality of products and services, and how the work is done.
Change: There is a reluctance to change the way things have always been done.	1 2 3 4 5 6 7	**Change**: Members view change as a way of life and an opportunity to excel in an ever-changing environment.
Resistance: Change tends to be planned and rolled out to members with little involvement and minimum communication.	1 2 3 4 5 6 7	**Resistance**: Members are actively involved in effecting change, which creates an understanding of why it is important and brings clarity to the new direction.
Processes: There is a lack of consistency in how members approach their work and orient new members.	1 2 3 4 5 6 7	**Processes**: Key work processes are documented and adhered to, to affect improvement and prevent re-work; they serve as the basis for orienting new members.
Changing Requirements: There is little time and effort invested in understanding and meeting changing internal and external requirements.	1 2 3 4 5 6 7	**Changing Requirements**: Members continually seek to understand and meet both external and internal wants, needs, and expectations.
Closing Gaps: Members are more inclined to address existing problems than look for new and innovative ways to improve how the work is done.	1 2 3 4 5 6 7	**Closing Gaps**: Members are skilled at assessing where they are, identifying where they need to be, and developing actions to close the gaps.
Benchmarking: Members are reluctant to consider solutions that are "not developed here."	1 2 3 4 5 6 7	**Benchmarking**: Best practices are sought out, researched, and utilized to affect change in a timely and efficient manner.
Planning and Implementing: Plans are limited or lack assigned responsibilities and time frames for holding members accountable for achieving desired results.	1 2 3 4 5 6 7	**Planning and Implementing**: Comprehensive plans are developed, implemented, and monitored to consistently achieve desired results.
Applying Measures: Members seldom apply methods for monitoring and measuring progress to gauge performance against desired outcomes.	1 2 3 4 5 6 7	**Applying Measures**: Members consistently apply both progress and result measures for gauging performance against desired outcomes.
Monitoring Progress: There is not a process for tracking and monitoring progress and performance against desired outcomes.	1 2 3 4 5 6 7	**Monitoring Progress**: Members regularly utilize measures to understand and celebrate progress against achieving desired outcomes and performance.

Where does your organization or team need to focus?

To pinpoint which factors need work to support continuous improvement, review your assessment and enter the three highest-rated and lowest-rated factors below.

Which three Contributing Factors did you rate the highest? (closest to seven)	Which three Contributing Factors did you rate the lowest? (closest to one)
1.	
2.	
3.	

Next Steps

- For those contributing factors rated the highest, keep doing what you are doing.
- For those contributing factors rated the lowest, take action to address them.

If you completed the self-assessment on your own and found value in the exercise, consider expanding the self-assessment to include other members of the organization or team. For example:

1. Have the Executive Team complete the self-assessment on the organization.
2. Compile and summarize their ratings on a single, blank assessment sheet.
3. Utilize the assessment summary as the basis for discussion.
4. Delegate responsibility for developing plans and actions to existing teams or standing committees.
5. You may also choose to commission a task force to take charge of the planning process for a specific set of contributing factors.

Expanding involvement provides additional insights, commitment and support, which contributes to an environment of continuous improvement throughout the organization.

If you have multiple teams or departments that you would like to participate in the self-assessment process, contact us at www.businesspaths.net to learn more about our on-line assessment services.

Embrace change as a business norm

Many experts have said that, when organizations fail to embrace change, they will fail to exist. Why? Because success in business today means affecting change...increasing revenue, responding to changing customer requirements, delivering new or improved products and services, growing and developing personnel, to name a few. Regardless of the challenges your organization faces, the volume of change can seem staggering.

Change has become a constant in today's business environment. Therefore, settling for the status quo is simply not an option. How can you keep up with the pace of change? Organizations need everyone searching for new and innovative ways to improve how the work is done and performance is achieved. Though it may sound easy, don't be fooled. Not everyone will gladly support and embrace change.

Overcome resistance to change

Does your organization initiate and lead change or impose it on your people? It's not hard to guess which approach generates the most resistance.

As mentioned earlier in the chapter, typically 20 percent of people support change. They believe it's time for the change and the right thing to do, while 50 percent will "wait and see." They need answers to the questions outlined below to determine where they stand. Then, 30 percent of the people oppose the change. They feel that the change is unnecessary or believe they will be negatively impacted by it.

You may never get this 30 percent to embrace the need for change. So, focus your time on reinforcing those who support the change and winning over the 50 percent on the fence. These two groups, combined, will give you a strong majority of people who will support the change and help make it a success.

As you communicate the need for the change, here's what people will ask or wonder about:

- Why are we doing this? Why now?
- What impact will it have on how we operate?
- How is it different from the way we do things today?
- How will it affect my job? My performance? My pay?
- Will it make things better or worse?
- What's in it for me?
- Am I capable of doing this?
- What if this doesn't work?

If these questions go unanswered, uncertainty, fear, and doubt will prevail. To minimize resistance and successfully bring about the needed change, you need to provide answers to these questions. And, if you involve your people, rather than imposing change on them, you will minimize resistance. How effectively you model and manage change will affect the level of resistance that you encounter.

When change becomes a routine part of doing business, it becomes much easier to introduce change and engage your people in finding new and innovative ways to make a difference.

Avoid pitfalls to change

John Kotter in his book, *Leading Change* cites eight errors that people make when trying to tackle change. Keep these errors in mind, and do what you can to avoid them, as you plan and implement change.

#	Error	How to avoid the error
1	Not establishing a great enough sense of urgency	Select the critical few areas that need focus and action. Those with the highest payback will drive the greatest sense of urgency.
2	Not creating a powerful enough guiding coalition	Identify people who will help make the change a reality, and gain their support and cooperation for the effort.
3	Lack of Vision for change	Create and articulate your vision for change.
4	Undercommunicating the Vision by a factor of 10	Use every available method to share your vision and strategy. Ensure that the people leading the change effort model behaviors that support the effort.
5	Not removing obstacles to the new Vision	Empower and support your people as they take risks, apply creative ideas, and change systems to achieve the desired result.
6	Not systematically planning for and creating short-term wins	Make sure to gauge progress and celebrate successes throughout the process. This will help keep the process moving along.
7	Declaring victory too soon	Be patient. Changes in one area may drive the need for change in another. In the event that happens, address other conditions as they arise. A lot of wonderful plans get abandoned prematurely because they are not given adequate time to succeed.
8	Not anchoring changes in the Corporation's culture	People need to understand how the change supports organizational success. They also need to know the issue has substance and reflects more than a "current fad."

Begin with key work processes

The place to begin your continuous improvement and change efforts is with key work processes. List your team or organization's key work processes below, and answer the two follow-on questions:

Key work process:	Does it consistently deliver results? Yes / No	Are steps in the work process documented? Yes / No

If you have documented work processes that consistently deliver results, congratulations! If some are documented but fail to deliver consistent results—what an opportunity for a continuous improvement effort! If you find undocumented work processes, get them documented now!

The easiest way I have found to get a work process documented is to have the people who actually use the work process write each step of the work process on a Post-It Note. Then have them arrange the Post-It Notes in the order on a flip chart or other large surface. Post-Its make it easy for the group to review them, and move them around, until they have the steps in an order all users agree to.

Now, document them in a list format or on a flow chart for use as a reference for employees and a training aid for new employees.

I have found when a work process is documented, but not delivering results, one of two conditions exist:

1. The agreed upon work process steps are not consistently being followed.
2. The process, as it exists, cannot deliver consistent results, so the process needs modification.

Both situations provide opportunities for continuous improvement efforts or problem solving.

Plan for change and improvement efforts

When you take the time to plan for change and actively involve your people in affecting that change, their efforts should yield strong results. As people become more comfortable being involved in improvement efforts, they will get in the habit of anticipating what is possible and take the action necessary to make it a reality. These types of proactive efforts end up being received and accepted much easier than having change imposed in response to a crisis or problem.

What critical few areas need to change on your team or in your organization? Enter them below.

Focus of change:
Example: We need increased leadership and empowerment

1.

_____

2.

_____

3.

_____

Decide who will participate in planning the effort

Pick one of the focus areas from your list and decide who will participate in the change or continuous improvement effort. The following questions will help with your selection:

        a. Who are the internal customers for the plan?

        b. Who will represent other people affected by this plan?

        c. Will this plan affect external customers? If so, how?

        d. What support resources do you need for implementation?

Once you have the participants selected, the planning process can begin. Participant involvement throughout the process provides invaluable input and gains their commitment to the final plan. You may choose to have them share the status of the plan with their peers and gather input for use during the planning process.

Focus of change:	Planning participants:
Example: Increased leadership and empowerment	Volunteers from each leadership team Human Resource Director Representative from Executive Team President/CEO
The one you decided to start with:	

Take Action—Call for a "power10"!

Let the planning begin

You now have commissioned your task force. When you pull them together, explain why you have formed the group and share and discuss the change you believe needs to be made. Let them know if the task force is serving in a decision-making or a recommending capacity. If they have decision-making authority, share any boundaries you expect them to work within.

Complete a gap analysis

The continuous improvement approach I recommend begins with a Gap Analysis. As you conduct a Gap Analysis, you will identify gaps between where you are today and where you need to be in the future in either a process and/or performance. Then you will develop a transition plan designed to close those gaps.

Here is an overview of gap analysis:

Focus of Change: _____

Challenges/Opportunities: **Future state/Goals:**

_____   _____

_____   _____

_____   _____

You will find a Gap Analysis Worksheet and example at the end of this chapter for your use. Here are the steps to follow:

- First, enter the area that you have identified as needing improvement on the worksheet.
- Second, identify major challenges or opportunities that exist in this focus area.
- Third, establish the Future State/Goal you want to achieve.
- Fourth, explore where you are (current state) today relative to the Future State/Goal.
- Fifth, clarify the where you need to be (desired state).

A key part of gap analysis focuses on the contrast between where you are and where you need to be. When you establish and compare the current state to the desired state, pinpointing actions to close the gaps becomes much easier and effective.

Clarifying where you need to be also provides an additional benefit. It allows the future to "pull" participants as they develop plans and actions. Without a picture of where you need to be, people's own perceptions can become limiting factors in planning for change. Having the future "pull" during the planning process versus having the past "push" sets the stage for achieving greater improvement in less time.

Develop a Transition Plan to close the gaps

With the gaps clarified, it's time to develop a Transition Plan for closing the gaps between the current and desired states. You will find a blank Transition Plan and example at the end of this chapter for your use.

Here are the steps to follow:

1) Develop specific actions that, when implemented, will close the gaps and allow achievement of the future states/goals that you established. You may find instances where exploring and implementing best practices will be the most effective way to address a given area.

2) Assign a point person, responsible for ensuring that assigned actions get implemented.

3) Establish completion dates for each action.

4) Determine what measures (metrics) you will use to gauge progress and success.

The Transition Plan becomes a working document for conducting progress checks. At scheduled follow-up sessions, each person assigned responsibility for overseeing specific actions should provide a status on the progress and success of his or her area of responsibility.

When all actions have been implemented and desired results achieved, update your standard operating procedures to include the new work processes.

Congratulations! You have successfully improved how the work is done or performance is achieved.

Continuous Improvement

Insights:	Tips:
<ul><li>Many forces drive organizational change.</li><li>Change should be considered a normal part of business.</li><li>Continuous improvement should be part of the organization's fabric.</li><li>People working together can accomplish great things.</li></ul>	<ul><li>Function in your role of change agent.</li><li>Get everyone seeking new and innovative ways for how the work is done and performance is achieved.</li><li>Planning for change increases its effectiveness and minimizes resistance.</li><li>Document key work processes to support continuous improvement efforts.</li></ul>

For information about available products and services visit www.businesspaths.net

Focus of Change: _____

Future State/Goal: _____

Challenges/Opportunities:

1. _____
2. _____
3. _____

Desired State:

○   ○   ○   ○   ○   ○

Transition Plan

Current State:

○   ○   ○   ○   ○   ○

Focus of Change EXAMPLE: Increased Leadership and Empowerment

Challenges/Opportunities:

1. Investing more time and energy leading

2. Increasing the level of empowerment

Future State/Goal:

- Devote 70-90% of our time to leading

- Functional areas effectively manage their day-to-day business

Desired State:

Our time and energy is focused on strategy, partnering, and promoting organizational development.

There is a clear sense of direction, and members of the organization are actively working toward the attainment of common goals.

Roles and responsibilities are well understood, and members of the organization are comfortable making decisions that affect their work.

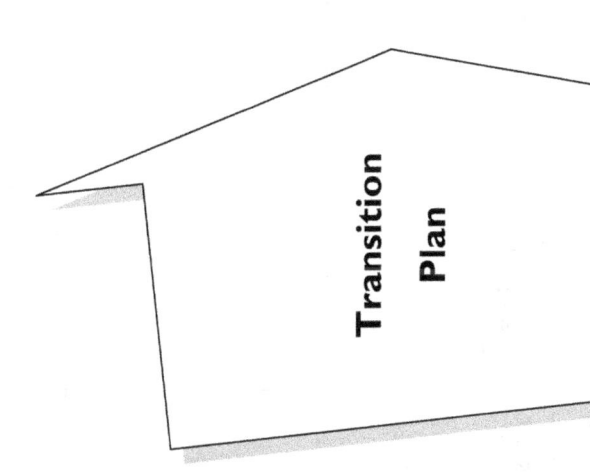

Transition Plan

Current State:

The Leadership Team's time is consumed solving day-to-day operational issues.

Priorities and focus are unclear or not understood.

People don't know or are uncertain about their roles, responsibilities, and decision aurhority.

Transition Plan

Focus for Change: _____

Future State/Goal: _____

Plans and Actions	Responsible Person(s)	Planned/ Actual Completion	Measure(s)	Status:

Transition Plan – *EXAMPLE* -

Focus for Change: Increased Leadership and Empowerment

Future State/Goal: Devote 70-90% of our time leading; functional areas effectively manage their day-to-day business

Plans and Actions	Responsible Person(s)	Planned/ Actual Completion	Measure(s)	Status:
Schedule time to review where we are and determine where we need to be.	President	by 4/15	Overview developed	
Present overview.	President	4/24 Staff Meeting	Management Team is refocused on where we're heading.	
Take a leadership inventory.	President, Managers	5/9 Workshop	Participants have identified 2-3 leadership focus areas and developed actions for implementation.	
Clarify roles and responsibilities; understand functional-area needs and develop next steps.	President, Managers	5/22 Staff Meeting	Roles and responsibilities are documented, including decision authority; plans and actions are established to meet developmental needs.	

Communication

Share openly, listen actively, and communicate honestly

What do you believe is your most important role as a manager or leader? Communication, communication, communication.

Just as the Coxswain must maintain a high level of clarity to keep his or her crew moving forward in the race, your ability to gain trust and build sound relationships depends on the effectiveness of your communication. Think about it…whether talking to a customer, negotiating with a supplier, or working with your people, communication provides the basis for all interaction and understanding.

You set the tone and create an environment of openness and trust for your team or organization. And, if you want your people to share their thoughts and opinions and exchange information and knowledge, it begins with you.

Your leadership and communication will determine how engaged your people are in their work and their level of commitment to overall success. Whether they need direction, motivation, clarity, your time, honesty, understanding, etc., the primary skill you deploy is…communication. This is true whether you are:

- Clarifying direction
- Setting expectations
- Discussing problems and potential solutions
- Providing coaching
- Conducting meetings
- Sharing feedback
- Recognizing performance contributions

What's happening in reality?

In a Ken Blanchard Group study of fourteen hundred leaders and managers, here's how they rated communication and management responsibilities:

43 percent feel the most critical skill of a leader is communicating and listening

41 percent feel inappropriate use of communication or listening is the biggest mistake leaders make

82 percent feel leaders and mangers fail to provide appropriate feedback

81 percent fail to listen or involve others in the process

76 percent fail to set clear goals and objectives

Nearly 6 of 10 fail to train and develop their people

Unfortunately, I am not surprised with these results. During my years in management consulting, communication posed the single greatest challenge for organizations, departments, and teams. With communication being such an integral part of our lives, why have people failed to master it…even after years of practice?

The need for effective communication has increased over the past few decades, with the shift toward collaboration, empowerment, teams, and partnerships. Conversations once held between managers and their direct reports now take place amongst team members, cross functional groups, and strategic partners. This increase in communication is critical to successfully address the ongoing challenges that organizations face, both today and in the future.

The availability and dissemination of information has long been a topic of discussion in many organizations. For many years, information was kept and shared only at senior-management levels. Decisions were made at the management level, and employees were expected to implement the programs and changes handed down.

The dissemination of information was born as people got involved in running the day-to-day business and decision-making moved closer to the customer. The questions became, "What information should be shared?" "With whom?" "Do we run the risk of proprietary information falling into the wrong hands?" "How much, and what information do members of the organization need to do their jobs effectively?"

And, now, the questions surround the many forms of communication. "What technology should we include in our communication infrastructure? Do social media have a place in our ongoing communication needs? What boundaries do we need to put in place to ensure technology adds value to our organization?

An excellent way to maximize communication is to develop and implement a communication plan.

How effective is communication throughout your organization?

Take a few minutes to complete the following self-assessment.

First, decide which group you will assess. The organization? A department? A team? Now, keep this group "top of mind," as you proceed through the self-assessment. Your ratings will identify conditions that contribute to effective communication and pinpoint areas that need additional focus and attention.

The Self-Assessment includes ten pairs of statements that represent factors that contribute to establishing and maintaining a sound communication process. Read the statement in the left-hand and right-hand column for each contributing factor. Place an "x" on the scale of one to seven that indicates where you view the team, department, or organization *today* in relationship to the two statements. If you find that part of the description rates higher and part lower, plot the lower rating on the scale of one to seven.

Here is an example of one pair of statements, and the rating scale:

CONTRIBUTING FACTOR:	WHERE WE ARE	WHERE WE NEED TO BE
Communication: Communication is guarded, resulting in minimal involvement in addressing and resolving issues.	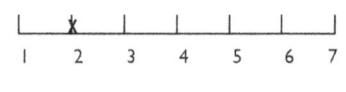	**Communication:** A high level of openness and honesty allows members to share information, ideas, and opinions to address and resolve issues

If you decided to have other people participate in the self-assessment process, keep this in mind: People generally believe that their team or organization falls into a high-performing category. However, when I have facilitated the self-assessment process, I've noticed that, as groups review the summary of their individual ratings, they are astonished to find they've rated themselves extremely low. They even suggest that they must have been thinking about the organization when they applied the rating—certainly not their team.

When this situation became a barrier to moving forward with plans and actions to improve the team's effectiveness, I had them retake the self-assessment, being sure to focus on their team or group. In every situation, the overall ratings came out the same or lower than the original assessment.

The moral of the story:

- Ensure that everyone participating in the self-assessment is clear about which group he or she is assessing.
- Assure them that the overall assessment simply provides a starting point for developing plans and implementing actions that will increase the team or group's effectiveness.

If participants tell you, "It's tough settling on a rating," it's likely they feel that the group does well against some parts of the description and not so well against

others. As a result, they have a tough time assigning a rating. Share the following example, which will help them feel more comfortable applying a rating.

> *As you read the statements in the left-hand and right-hand columns, let's say you believe that overall employee communication is guarded (a 2 rating), but managers seem to be honest in their communication (a 5 rating). Members share little responsibility for addressing issues (a 3 rating). There is a need for more open communication (a 2 rating). You just came up with two 2s one 3, and one 5 rating.*
>
> *As you select an overall rating for this contributing Factor, "err on the low side" to ensure that areas receiving 2 and 3 ratings get addressed. In this example, you may choose to give Communication an overall rating of 2.5*

Now, take a few minutes to complete the "power10" self-assessment on the following page for your organization or team.

*Communication Assessment for:*_____

(i.e. ABC Company, Sales Department, Financial Team)

Read the statements in the left-hand and right-hand columns for each of the ten Contributing Factors. Place an "x" on the scale of one to seven that indicates where you view the team, department, or organization *today* in relationship to the two statements.

CONTRIBUTING FACTOR	WHERE WE ARE	WHERE WE NEED TO BE
Communication: Communication is guarded, resulting in minimal involvement in addressing and resolving issues.	1 2 3 4 5 6 7	**Communication:** A high level of openness and honesty allows members to share information, ideas, and opinions to address and resolve issues.
Planning: There is a lack of planning to keep lines of communication open and provide the information members need to perform successfully.	1 2 3 4 5 6 7	**Planning:** There is an established communication plan designed to foster open communication and provide timely and quality information to members.
Interaction: There is a reluctance to share information and a lack of the skills required to bring clarity and common understanding to discussions.	1 2 3 4 5 6 7	**Interaction:** Members effectively share and exchange information with each other, test their understanding, and summarize key points of discussions.
Listening: Members tend to communicate their own views, showing little interest in understanding or clarifying other members' points of view.	1 2 3 4 5 6 7	**Listening:** Members actively listen to each other's points of view and convey their understanding, enabling effective two-way communication.
Conflict: Members avoid discussing and addressing potential conflicts that arise.	1 2 3 4 5 6 7	**Conflict:** Differing views and opinions are openly shared and discussed to reach mutually satisfying outcomes.
Skills: There is a lack of focus and training on the skills required to maximize the effectiveness of ongoing communication.	1 2 3 4 5 6 7	**Skills:** Members regularly demonstrate their effectiveness in listening, verbal, written, presentation, and non-verbal skills.
Information: The information members need to effectively perform their job is not readily available or accessible.	1 2 3 4 5 6 7	**Information:** Members consistently receive and have access to the information they need to do their jobs.
Meetings: There is significant time invested in meetings with minimum pay-back due to an inadequate planning and an absence of strong facilitation.	1 2 3 4 5 6 7	**Meetings:** Meetings act as an effective means of sharing and processing information, which allows members to actively participate in overall success.
Inclusion: Members are expected to carry out plans and actions that are established without their input or involvement.	1 2 3 4 5 6 7	**Inclusion:** Members are actively involved in planning and implementing actions that affect overall success.
Trust: There is little trust and limited cooperation amongst the members.	1 2 3 4 5 6 7	**Trust:** There is a high level of trust and cooperation, resulting in win-win outcomes.

Where does your organization or team need to focus?

To pinpoint which factors need work to enhance communication, review your assessment and enter the three highest-rated and lowest-rated factors below.

Which three Contributing Factors did you rate the highest? (closest to seven)	Which three Contributing Factors did you rate the lowest? (closest to one)
1.	
2.	
3.	

Next Steps

- For those contributing factors rated the highest, keep doing what you are doing.
- For those contributing factors rated the lowest, take action to address them.

If you completed the self-assessment on your own and found value in the exercise, consider expanding the self-assessment to include other members of the organization or team. For example:

1. Have the Executive Team complete the self-assessment on the organization.
2. Compile and summarize their ratings on a single, blank assessment sheet.
3. Utilize the assessment summary as the basis for discussion.
4. Delegate responsibility for developing plans and actions to existing teams or standing committees.
5. You may also choose to commission a task force to take charge of the planning process for a specific set of contributing factors.

Expanding involvement provides additional insights, commitment, and support, which contributes to the effectiveness of communication throughout the organization.

If you have multiple teams or departments that you would like to participate in the self-assessment process, contact us at www.businesspaths.net to learn more about our on-line assessment services.

The basics of communication

Why is communication important? It serves as the basis for building relationships and trust...two critical attributes for developing successful teams and organizations.

Whether you communicate with one person or address a team or group, you are sharing, gathering, or processing thoughts and/or information. You use one or more of four communication skills: verbal, written, presentation, and non-verbal. And, based on the situation, your interchange will involve one or more forms of communication, including voice, written/print, or digital. Here are some examples:

One-way communication:

- Voice   Feedback, certain meeting topics, presentations, radio promotion
- Written/print   Memos, reports, policies, newsletters, promotional materials
- Digital   Voice mail, email, blogs, social media, websites, some text messages, tweets

Two-way communication:

- Voice   Face-to-face dialogue, phone calls, group discussions, problem solving, negotiation
- Written/print   Some surveys
- Digital   Information gathering emails, blogs, LinkedIn, Facebook, My Space, some text messages,

In order for one-way communication to be effective, you need to answer an important question that readers have, "What's in it for me?" Effective two-way communication requires active listening...the single most important communication skill. Sounds pretty simple, doesn't it? Then, why do people have such difficulty mastering this vital skill?

Barriers to effective two-way communication

Two general barriers get in the way of effective two-way communication, attitude and approach. Here are some examples of each and ways to overcome these barriers:

Attitude

Examples of barriers:
- I know better than you do
- My ideas make the most sense
- We don't have time for this
- Being a problem identifier vs. problem solver
- Choosing to not communicate
- Win-lose vs. win-win

How to overcome these barriers:
- Actively work to build trust
- Show an interest in others' needs
- Work toward mutual benefit

Approach

Examples of barriers:
- Failing to actively listen
- Avoiding conflict
- Focus on own position vs. mutual interests
- Assuming what others need vs. asking
- Judging people vs. focusing on the problem
- Hidden agendas
- Emotional outbursts

How to overcome these barriers:
- Listen actively
- Understand your audience
- Work to get your message across

Take Action—Here's a "power10" for you!

Listen up!

Many people say we have one mouth and two ears for a good reason…to spend more time listening and less time talking. As mentioned at the beginning of this chapter, fourteen hundred managers who responded to a Ken Blanchard survey believe the following:

43 percent feel the most critical skill of a leader is communicating and listening.
41 percent feel inappropriate use of communication or listening is the biggest mistake leaders make.

How effective a listener are you? To gain insight, assess how frequently you exhibit the following behaviors:

Behavior	Never	Seldom	Sometimes	Often
I tend to talk more than I listen.				
I find myself thinking about what I'm going to say next.				
I get impatient waiting for the other person to finish talking.				
I interrupt people when they are talking.				
I respond before the person has finished speaking.				
I find my mind wandering to other subjects.				

If you have opportunities for improvement, here are a few steps you can take to become a more active listener:

1. Stop what you are doing and look at the person.
2. Concentrate on what they are saying and avoid distractions.
3. Listen carefully to understand the whole message.
4. Ask open-ended questions to gain clarification.
5. Watch for non-verbal signals from the person speaking
6. Test your understanding before you respond
7. Share pertinent input on the topic
8. Summarize any conclusions or agreements that are made

When you follow these steps, you will become a more active listener and therefore a more effective communicator.

Say the words

Effective communication poses many challenges for people. One significant challenge for most people is that they struggle to simply "say the words." They are reluctant to speak openly and honestly for fear of hurting someone's feelings, causing conflict, or generating an emotional response. As a result, important exchanges fail to happen.

As a leader, how can you help your people become the best they can be if you are unwilling to communicate openly and honestly? You need to be an "honest broker" in all areas of the business, as well as share where your people need to improve, assist with their growth, and provide feedback on their development.

> **When your intent is to develop your people to be the best they can be, "saying the words" comes easily.**

I remember taking over responsibility for a new organization. And, as I was getting to know the people who worked with and for me on various teams, one woman stood out above the rest. She was unbelievably effective at her job. I found out that she was blessed with a photographic memory, which made a huge difference in her ability to function in her role. She was an invaluable resource for all the members of the organization, as a result of this wonderful gift.

Unfortunately, her communication left much to be desired. The content of her exchanges was always accurate, but her approach was direct, often brash and demeaning. Her exchanges left those on the receiving end feeling stupid and licking their wounds. Her behavior was a barrier to building a successful team. It also left many people from other parts of the organization with the perception that the department was unsupportive of the greater effort. There was no question that this situation had to change.

I made a few informal calls and found that her impact had been felt before. But, in reviewing her employee file, there was no indication that her behavior had been formally addressed during her fourteen years of employment. Rather than dealing with the issue, managers moved her from organization to organization or simply created new jobs to put her in. They failed to "say the words" that would help this woman be the best she could be and develop and grow in her career!

I sat down with her and we talked about the negative impact her behavior was having on those around her. We talked about what she wanted to accomplish in her career. I shared my expectations. And we came to agreement on actions she would take to bring her behavior into line with my expectations. We also settled on "silent signals" I would send her if I observed situations where she was reverting back to her old ways.

Her progress was remarkable. She had totally dedicated herself to changing her ways. I remember one time, as we sat down to discuss how she was doing, tears welled up in her eyes. And, as they began rolling down her face, she thanked me for getting involved. She also told me that I was the first manager in all her years of employment that cared enough to invest the time to help her grow and develop in her career.

When leaders are reminded that developing their people to be the best they can be is one of their primary roles, "saying the words" becomes much easier.

Address conflict as it happens

No matter how much you might hope that if you avoid conflict it will go away, it won't. Don't be fooled. It will simply lie dormant...until the next time...when it erupts!

There are a number of things that generate conflict, ranging from personality conflicts to a lack of communication itself. You might find that misunderstandings or diverse points of view are the culprits. Or different styles that cause mixed signals may be to blame. Regardless of the cause, the more skilled you are at addressing conflict, the more room there will be for open and honest communication. So, let's take a look at steps you can take to address conflict situations as they happen.

Important things to remember as you facilitate conflict resolution:

- Your goal is to hear all sides.
- You need to listen objectively vs. placing blame.
- You need to ask open-ended questions to draw out various points of view.
- Each person's perception is their reality.
- Before a solution can be found, feelings need to be shared, followed by getting the facts on the table.

Here are some steps that will help you effectively address conflict:

1. Bring everyone together.
2. Establish ground rules (i.e., openness and honesty, everyone is heard, listen without reacting, positive attitudes, share facts and specific behaviors to support opinions and feelings).
3. Define the conflict.
4. Hear all sides of the story.
5. Draw out and process emotions.
6. Ask for job-related specifics.
7. Offer feedback, paraphrasing what you have heard.
8. Gain commitment to jointly resolving the issue.
9. Establish goals for the resolution.
10. Establish agreed-upon actions for each issue.
11. Assign responsibility and establish a due date for each action.
12. Meet on a regular basis to review progress until goals are achieved.

When you follow these steps, resolving conflict will become much easier.

Conduct effective meetings

The amount of time spent in meetings is on the rise, and the number and duration of meetings is increasing. With the growing need for having everyone in the boat, actively rowing and collaborating, meetings have become an important and vital part of doing business. As a result, maximizing meeting effectiveness is key to optimizing overall productivity.

Here are some interesting statistics from a variety of sources:

- Managers and knowledge workers estimate that 25 to 80 percent of their time is spent in meetings.
- As much as 67 percent of time spent in meetings is wasted.
- Having no goals or agenda is the second most commonly reported meeting problem.*
- Nearly one half of meetings do not have a written agenda.**
- 73 percent of respondents feel that an agenda is "essential" for a productive meeting.**

*Moswick and Nelson survey of 950 managers and professionals

** Harrison-Hofstra survey

Build a meeting agenda

Many factors affect how productive meetings are…the size of the group, set-up of the room, skills of the facilitator, preparation for the meeting, to mention a few. Sometimes meetings are held simply because there is a standard meeting date and time established. Regardless of all the variables, the one thing that enhances meeting effectiveness is the development and use of an agenda.

The following is an example of a recommended agenda format. There is also a blank agenda at the end of this chapter. Several things about this agenda format enhance meeting effectiveness:

- Stating the purpose of the meeting lets people know why they are coming together.

- Clarifying whether an agenda item involves sharing or requires processing helps participants prepare accordingly.

- Sharing the desired outcome of each item allows everyone to know what needs to be accomplished.

- There is space at the bottom to note any decisions and actions, so copies can be made and distributed at the conclusion of the meeting.

Meeting Agenda - *EXAMPLE*

Leadership Team Meeting	**Date:** Monday, January 5th	**Start Time:** 8:30 a.m.
	Location: Conference Room	**Stop Time:** 10:00 a.m.

Meeting Purpose: Develop a Communication Plan for the organization

Agenda Item	S/P	Desired Outcome	Facilitator / Presenter	Time Allotted
Communication Plan concept	S	Everyone understands the value of having a Communication Plan.	CEO	10 minutes
Information and communication needs	S/P	Build a list of information and communication that employees need to perform successfully.	CEO / All Team Members	30 minutes
How, when, who will provide information and meet communication needs	P	Finalize a Communication Plan for the organization.	CEO	40 minutes
Wrap up	S	Understand what's been accomplished; establish next steps.	CEO	10 minutes

S = Sharing Item; P = Processing Item

Decision/Action:	Person Responsible:	By When:
Share the Communication Plan with all teams	All managers	End of the month

Develop and implement a communication plan

The most important skill a manager can possess is communication. The single greatest challenge of the organizations I've worked with over the years is communication. Effective communication provides the basis for building relationships and trust. And the list goes on. Yet most people in management positions do not have a communication plan. It's time to fix that!

The place to start is to determine the what, why, how, when and who of communication. Spell it out in a communication plan, follow it consistently and reap the rewards!

Begin with understanding people's needs

What information/communication do your people need? Take a look at how your organization is structured, and decide how you want to tackle a needs analysis.

Take the time to list what information/communication your employees need:
Here's an example:

Organizational Level	Department/Team Level	Individual Level
• Headquarters/Board direction, insights	• Day-to-day operations	• What's expected
• Organizational direction	• Performance expectations	• How to do the job
• Ongoing performance	• Actual performance	• Decision authority they have
• General industry information	• Agreed upon work processes	• How they can make a difference
• Policies and procedures	• Kudos/Recognition	• Ongoing feedback and coaching
	• What is happening in other departments/on other teams	• Performance Review
		• Professional development

Now, using what you've identified, complete the Communication Plan at the end of this chapter by:

1. Entering each of them on the communication plan.

2. Determining what vehicle will be used to deliver the information/communication.

3. Deciding the frequency of delivery.

4. Assigning responsibility for who will deliver it.

Congratulations! You are on your way to having a comprehensive communication plan. Once it is complete, plot each of the activities on your calendar and/or a shared Calendar of Events. Review the calendar on a regular basis, and plan ahead for sharing the information and effectively communicating with your people. They are counting on you to ensure they get what they need to be successful in their jobs and help the organization achieve its goals!

Volumes have been written on communication. This chapter focuses on the critical few areas that will get you on your way to more effective communication.

Communication	
Insights:	**Tips:**
• Communication is a significant challenge for most organizations. • Most people have not mastered effective communication. • Communication is a leader's most important skill. • People seldom remember what they are told only once. • Agendas increase meeting effectiveness.	• Communicate, communicate, communicate. • People need information to be fully engaged. • Listen more, talk less. • Say the words. • Address conflict as it happens.

For information about available products and services visit www.businesspaths.net

Meeting Agenda				
Organization/Department/Team		**Date:** **Location:**		**Start Time:** **Stop Time:**
Meeting Purpose:				
Agenda Item	**S/P**	**Desired Outcome**	**Facilitator / Presenter**	**Time Allotted**
❑				
❑				
❑				
❑				
❑				
❑				

S = Sharing Item; P = Processing Item

Decision/Action:	Person Responsible:	By When:

Communication Plan

Organizational Level

What information?	How it will be delivered	Frequency of delivery	Who will deliver it?

Department/Team Level

What information?	How it will be delivered	Frequency of delivery	Who will deliver it?

Individual Level

What information?	How it will be delivered	Frequency of delivery	Who will deliver it?

Communication Plan - *Example*

Organizational Level

What information?	How it will be delivered	Frequency of delivery	Who will deliver it?
Headquarters/Board direction & insights	Organizational meeting Email President's report to staff	Quarterly Monthly	CEO Executive Assistant
Organizational direction	Organizational meeting	Quarterly	CEO
Ongoing performance	Organizational meeting	Quarterly	CEO
General industry information			
Policies and procedures			

Department/Team Level

What information?	How it will be delivered	Frequency of delivery	Who will deliver it?
Day-to-day operations	Team meetings	Weekly	Manager
Performance expectations	Team meeting	First of year	Manager
Actual performance	Team meetings	Weekly/Monthly	Manager
Agreed upon work processes	Work group meetings	First of year; New personnel added	Work group leader
Kudos/Recognition	Team meetings	Monthly	Manager
What's new in other departments/on other teams?	Team meetings Newsletter	Weekly Monthly	Manager Publisher

Individual Level

What information?	How it will be delivered	Frequency of delivery	Who will deliver it?
What's expected?	One-on-one	Beginning of year	Manager
How to do the job	Training	As required	Trainers
Decision authority individual has	One-on-one	Reviewed at beginning of year; updated as changes	Manager
How they can make a difference?	One-on-one	Monthly	Manager
Ongoing feedback and coaching	One-on-one	Monthly	Manager
Performance Review	One-on-one	Month after year-end	Manager
Professional development	Annual career guidance Review and Plan	Anniversary month Quarterly	Manager Manager

Learning and Growth

Develop your people to be the best they can be

Just as a Coxswain taps into the strengths of each crewmember to prepare for a team win, your job is to develop your people to be the best they can be. The people who work with and for you are your most valuable asset for meeting the challenges of today and tomorrow's changing environment.

Organizations have a lot on their plates. They need to figure out how to play in a global economy, search for ways to consistently deliver relevant products and services, develop new methods for staying on top of changing customer requirements, to name a few. They need their front-line employees to handle the day-to-day business and their managers to help address global implications, industry shifts, and competitive threats while leading their people.

Some organizations have moved decision-making closer to the customer to increase responsiveness to customer needs. Others have created and developed self-directed teams to shift responsibility for running the day-to-day business. Problem-solving and continuous improvement efforts have become the way organizations share responsibility and engage employees in improving how the work is done and how performance is achieved.

Shifts in responsibility like these drive the need to expand employee knowledge and skills. They also come with both good and bad news. The good news…employees and teams get more involved, learn more about the business, and become more invested in the outcome. The bad news…people are often given additional responsibility without the training they need to successfully handle the day-to-day business, develop and implement lasting solutions, and continuously improve how the work is done.

Reap the rewards

That said, you will reap many rewards when you commit to developing your people to be the best they can be. They will learn and grow, and you will enhance your leadership skills. You will find that your time frees up as your people become actively involved and take ownership for running the day-to-day business and continuously improving how the work is done. In addition, better decisions will be made, employee satisfaction will improve, motivation and commitment will increase, and manager-employee relationships will grow stronger.

As you tap into your people's creativity, develop and engage them, trust builds and they come together rowing in the same direction. They enjoy being part of a winning organization where they feel valued for their contributions. And their commitment to achieve organizational and team goals increases.

In order to enjoy this success, you must tap into your people's knowledge and creativity, willingly relinquish control, and trust that they will do the right thing when given the chance.

From personal experience I can tell you that there is nothing like:

- Seeing the "light bulbs" come on as your people learn and grow
- The pride you will feel when your people are successful
- Celebrating the promotion of one of your own
- The gratification you get when you receive a phone call from someone who worked for you years ago to say thank you for everything you did for them and that they owe their success to what they learned and experienced when they worked for you

Where are your priorities?

Unfortunately, since the early '90s organizations have fallen prey to bottom-line focus and short-term decision-making. They:

- Lost sight of the fact that their most valuable asset is their people
- Failed to recognize that the learning and growth of their employees is vital to addressing ongoing challenges
- Lost sight that professional growth and development means more than simply checking off a box when someone attends training
- Failed to provide the reinforcement and support their people need to successfully apply the concepts and theories they learned in training
- Shaved training and development budgets when times got tough

When they realize their short-term decisions have had a negative impact on success, it is too late.

The following statistics tell a sobering story about what happens when organizations fall behind in the development of their employees:

Impact on recruiting, productivity and leadership:

A survey of four hundred, twenty-five Senior Executives from leading organizations in North America, Europe, and Asia pinpointed these top three workforce priorities:

- Attracting and retaining a skilled staff
- Getting the best out of their people (improving performance)
- Developing employees into capable leaders

Impact on employee engagement:

- Only one in seven employees (14 percent) is fully engaged with their jobs and willing to go the extra mile for their company.
- People want to contribute more, but their leaders and supervisors put obstacles in their way.
- The majority of employees are moderately engaged at best, and 25 percent are actively disengaged.
- 55 percent of US respondents are open and vulnerable to other job offers.
- More than eight in ten engaged employees (80+ percent) believe they can positively impact the quality of their company's products, compared to one in three (33 percent) of those employees who are disengaged.
- Nearly three-fourths of highly engaged employees (75 percent) believe they can positively affect customer service compared to one fourth (25 percent) of those who are disengaged.
- Six of ten highly engaged employees (60 percent) planned to stay with their current employer versus one-fourth (25 percent) of those who are disengaged.

Towers Perrin survey of 85,000 employees in large and midsize companies in sixteen countries and four continents

Impact on preparing future leaders

- Most companies have leadership programs, but most are not executing them well.
- Only 57 percent of organizations have a strategy for selecting, rewarding, and developing leaders.
- Less than one third of companies measure their leadership programs' effectiveness.
- 43 percent of organizations track their high-potential leaders' turnover.

BusinessWire article, a Hewitt and Associates survey

Wow! These studies point out many opportunities in the area of learning and growth to take action and call for a *"power10"*!

With the complexities and challenges of today's business, investing in your people's learning and growth becomes essential to team and organizational success. It takes having everyone in the boat rowing the same direction to effectively navigate the waters and successfully arrive at the organization's desired destination.

How effectively does your organization train and develop its people?

Take a few minutes to complete the following self-assessment.

First, decide which group you will assess. The organization? A department? A team? Now, keep this group "top of mind," as you proceed through the self-assessment. Your ratings will identify conditions that contribute to an environment of learning and growth and pinpoint areas that need additional focus and attention.

The Self-Assessment includes ten pairs of statements that represent factors that contribute to an environment of learning and growth. Read the statement in the left-hand and right-hand column for each contributing factor. Place an "x" on the scale of one to seven that indicates where you view the team, department, or organization *today* in relationship to the two statements. If you find that part of the description rates higher and part lower, plot the lower rating on the scale of one to seven.

Here is an example of one pair of statements and the rating scale:

CONTRIBUTING FACTOR:	WHERE WE ARE	WHERE WE NEED TO BE
Learning and Growth: Members are protective of individual knowledge and are reluctant to share their expertise with others.	x 1 2 3 4 5 6 7	**Learning and Growth:** There is a strong commitment to continuous learning and knowledge-sharing to enhance overall effectiveness.

If you decide to have other people participate in the self-assessment process, please keep this in mind: People generally believe that their team or organization falls into a high-performing category. However, when I have facilitated the self-assessment process, I've noticed that, as groups review the summary of their individual ratings, they are astonished to find they've rated themselves extremely low. They even suggest that they must have been thinking about the organization when they applied the rating—certainly not their team.

When this situation became a barrier to moving forward with plans and actions to improve the team's effectiveness, I had them retake the self-assessment, being sure to focus on their team or group. In every situation, the overall ratings came out the same or lower than the original assessment.

The moral of the story:

- Ensure that everyone participating in the self-assessment is clear about which group he or she is assessing.

- Assure them that the overall assessment simply provides a starting point for developing plans and implementing actions that will increase the team or group's effectiveness.

If participants tell you, "It's tough settling on a rating," it's likely they feel that the group does well against some parts of the description and not so well against others. As a result, they have a tough time assigning a rating. Share the following example, which will help them feel more comfortable applying a rating.

As you read the statements in the left-hand and right-hand columns, let's say you believe that members are committed to learning and updating their skills (a 6 rating,) but the organization offers little to no supporting this area (a 1 rating). Members sometimes seem more comfortable keeping their knowledge and expertise to themselves (a 3 rating). Overall effectiveness appears unchanged (a 2 rating). You just came up with one 1, one 2, one 3, and one 6 rating.

As you select an overall rating for this contributing Factor, "err on the low side" to ensure that areas receiving 1 and 2 ratings get addressed. In this example, you may choose to give Learning and Growth an overall rating of 2.5

Now, take a few minutes to complete the "power10" self-assessment on the following page for your organization or team.

Learning and Growth Assessment for:_____

(i.e. ABC Company Sales Department, Finance Team)

Read the statements in the left-hand and right-hand columns for each of the ten Contributing Factors. Place an "x" on the scale of one to seven that indicates where you view the team, department, or organization *today* in relationship to the two statements.

CONTRIBUTING FACTOR	WHERE WE ARE	WHERE WE NEED TO BE
Learning and Growth: Members are protective of individual knowledge and are reluctant to share their expertise with others.	1 2 3 4 5 6 7	**Learning and Growth:** There is a strong commitment to continuous learning and knowledge-sharing to enhance overall effectiveness.
Skills Development: Members rely solely on the organization to provide the training they need to develop the skills necessary for success.	1 2 3 4 5 6 7	**Skills Development:** Members are committed to expanding their knowledge and updating their skills to meet current and future needs.
Career Development: There is not a defined process for assessing and developing member knowledge and skills.	1 2 3 4 5 6 7	**Career Development:** There is a formal and shared approach to developing the knowledge and skills required to perform successfully, as well as to prepare for advancement.
Skills Integration: There is not a defined method for reinforcing the application of newly acquired skills on the job.	1 2 3 4 5 6 7	**Skills Integration:** There is an effective method for reinforcing the application of skills and knowledge gained through training.
Competency: The knowledge, skills, and abilities required for positions are unclear or undefined.	1 2 3 4 5 6 7	**Competency:** The knowledge, skills, and abilities required for all positions are well defined and utilized as the basis for selection and development.
Training: There is little personal commitment to developing the knowledge and skills required to be successful.	1 2 3 4 5 6 7	**Training:** Members actively pursue opportunities to increase their knowledge and skills, and regularly participate in available training.
Technology: Members are reluctant to invest the needed time to keep current with new technology and software.	1 2 3 4 5 6 7	**Technology:** Members actively pursue opportunities to learn and apply the skills that keep them current with technology, updates, and system changes.
Information: The information members need to perform in their job is not readily available or accessible.	1 2 3 4 5 6 7	**Information:** The information members need to do their jobs is readily available to them in a usable format.
Added Responsibility: Members are often given additional responsibilities without the training or knowledge to perform them effectively.	1 2 3 4 5 6 7	**Added Responsibility:** As members are given new responsibilities, the infrastructure supports the skill development necessary to perform successfully.
Advancement: Positions are filled based more on who members know than demonstrated skills and abilities.	1 2 3 4 5 6 7	**Advancement:** There is a commitment to continuous learning and development that supports advancement to open positions.

Where does your organization or team need to focus?

To pinpoint which factors need work to embrace learning and growth, review your assessment and enter the three highest-rated and lowest-rated factors below.

Which three Contributing Factors did you rate the highest? (closest to seven)	Which three Contributing Factors did you rate the lowest? (closest to one)
1.	
2.	
3.	

Next Steps

- For those contributing factors rated the highest, keep doing what you are doing.
- For those contributing factors rated the lowest, take action to address them.

If you completed the self-assessment on your own and found value in the exercise, consider expanding the self-assessment to include other members of the organization or team. For example:

1. Have the Executive Team complete the self-assessment on the organization.
2. Compile and summarize their ratings on a single, blank assessment sheet.
3. Utilize the assessment summary as the basis for discussion.
4. Delegate responsibility to existing teams or standing committees for plan and action development.
5. You may also choose to commission a task force to take charge of the planning process for a specific set of contributing factors.

Expanding involvement provides additional insights, commitment, and support, which contributes to learning and growth throughout the organization.

If you have multiple teams or departments that you would like to participate in the self-assessment process, contact us at www.businesspaths.net to learn more about our on-line assessment services.

What support do you provide your most valuable asset?

Everyone in the organization has internal customers, whether they are their teammates, support staff, managers, etc. Internal customers are defined as those who need your output, information, or support to do their job.

As a leader in your organization, your *primary* internal customers are the people who report directly to you…your most valuable asset…your people. The relationship you build with your people is every bit as important as the relationship you have with external customers. They need your leadership and support to be successful. Also, it is when you work with and develop your people that you will succeed.

Your people are the primary face and voice to the external customer. *They* process customer requests and solve customer problems. *They* build customer confidence and trust in the organization. *Their* jobs exist because you single-handedly cannot accomplish all the work yourself. If you could, there would be no need for their positions.

So, whether you subscribe to the concepts of Transformational, Servant, Participative, or Situational Leadership, your job is to develop your people to be the best they can be. Through expectation setting, training and development, empowerment, ongoing coaching, and performance feedback, your people will thrive and you will be successful. Embracing this concept is not only your role, it is your responsibility.

Take Action—Here's a "power10" for you!

Clarify what your people need

Technology and the pace of change contribute significantly to the need for the ongoing learning and growth required in organizations today. Here are two startling statistics:

- The fund of information doubles every five years. *Information Anxiety*
- It only takes 3-5 years for 50% of people's skills to become outdated. *National Research Council*

Do you know what knowledge and skills your people need to successfully contribute to team and organizational success? The answer to this question should include a combination of what each of your people identify for himself or herself, as well as what you know are critical to their success. It is important to keep in mind that there is a progression of learning and growth that you need to take into consideration, because your people don't always know what they don't know.

Learning and growth progression:

Unaware	▶ Aware	▶ Learn	▶ Apply	▶ Perform
People don't realize what they don't know.	They realize what they don't know.	They are taught a new skill or behavior.	They begin putting the skill or behavior to use.	The skill or behavior becomes second nature.

What knowledge, skills, and abilities are required?

Today, organizations have a diverse set of workers that can range in age from eighteen to eighty. Some have a vast amount of business experience, having worked for many years. Others have a command of emerging technology, having grown up with technology at their fingertips. Their needs may be totally different as it relates to training and development, but the mix of experience can be used to build a strong learning and knowledge-sharing organization.

Take a moment to think about what it takes to grow the business, to compete in a global economy, to deliver consistent results. How will you ensure that your organization and employees are poised to deal with the challenges that lie ahead?

Though some people may be unhappy in their roles, I firmly believe everyone wants to do a good job. As a result, they want to feel valued for their contributions and be given an opportunity to learn and grow. However, in order for your people to be successful, they need to know what you expect, how to perform in their jobs, how they are doing against your expectations, and how they can make a difference for the team or organization. And it is your responsibility to ensure that they get what they need to be the best they can be.

Do you have a profile that outlines the knowledge, skills, and abilities that your people need to perform within their jobs, certifications that are required, and the source of that needed training? If so, congratulations! If not, take the time to put one together, using the Training and Development Needs Assessment form at the end of this chapter.

List the technical skills required to perform in a given job, as well as the soft skills needed to support the values of the organization. Here's an example:

Department/Function/Position:	Knowledge/Skills/Ability:
First line manager	<ul><li>Communication</li><li>Conflict management</li><li>Performance management</li><li>Performance evaluation</li><li>Empowerment</li><li>Problem solving</li><li>Continuous improvement</li><li>Team development</li><li>Leading change</li><li>Meeting effectiveness</li><li>Time management</li><li>Etc.</li></ul>

Once the knowledge, skills, and abilities are clarified, you have a framework for including available courses that will meet the team or organization's training and developmental needs.

Plan to get the bang for your training buck!

How you plan for delivery and follow-up of the training your people receive will have a significant impact on the return you get for your training dollars.

Some organizations simply check off the box as their people return from training. In cases like this, there is a "feel-good" approach to training…one where people feel good when they return from training, but seldom implement anything they were taught. This approach wastes people's valuable time and available training dollars.

Other organizations build an environment that supports learning and knowledge-sharing to keep pace and compete in their business community and specific industry. Some create learning camps to deepen the learning experience for their employees. Others include reinforcement and follow-up to ensure that their training investment pays dividends.

When you create an environment where your people continuously learn and grow, your team or organization is positioned to thrive in a highly-competitive environment.

Early in my consulting career, I developed and delivered customized training for business and industry clients on behalf of the local community college. As we discussed various projects, I made it clear that I had no interest in training people simply for the sake of training. I wanted participants to be able to apply what they learned when they returned to their jobs. So, we incorporated methods for ensuring follow-up that reinforced what was learned back in their workplace.

I believe it is very important for those in management to work with their people upon return from class to ensure that they can deepen their understanding and apply what was taught.

Ensure that your people can apply what was taught in training!

As you clarify your organization's training needs, explore the best way to get a bang for your training buck. Will it be by sending your people to external classes and seminars? Will you have managers provide some of the training? Do all people in management participate in the same training, so they can provide necessary reinforcement? Should you consider a train-the-trainer approach for consistency and follow-up? Will you use on-line, self-paced training, or Webinars to meet training needs?

Your role is to develop your people to be the best they can be. So, whichever approach you choose, make sure it does more than simply check off the training box. And remember, people want to be part of a winning organization and feel valued for their contributions. They want to do a good job, but need to know how to be successful…and their success becomes your success.

Make sure everyone has a professional development plan

In order for people to be successful, they need to know what's expected, have the skills to deliver performance against those expectations, and receive regular coaching and feedback on how they're doing. A key piece to delivering consistent results is building in accountability throughout the organization.

One way to ensure that members of your team or organization are focused on learning and growth is to ensure that every employee has a Professional Development Plan. Their plan needs to include actions that allow them to perform effectively in their current role, as well as developmental actions that prepare them for future positions.

Job related plans and actions

Every employee should be focused on professional development, whether they plan to remain in their current position or aspire to different positions or those requiring additional responsibility.

In the *Performance Management* chapter, my recommendation is that every person in a management position has his or her employees develop a professional action plan to help them successfully deliver against performance expectations. And, as your people implement their plan, meet with them on a regular basis to provide a status on their progress and ensure they modify their development plan if needed.

Career related plans and actions

How effective are you at building a bench of candidates to fill potential openings? For those employees interested in moving to other assignments or who are considered upwardly mobile, their professional action plan should include developmental actions that prepare them for the new assignment, as well as actions for successfully meeting their current performance expectations.

By providing the opportunity for continual learning and growth, ensuring that your people feel valued for their contributions, and the development of teams and partnerships, you build a framework for the organization and its employees to achieve success in today's highly competitive, dynamic environment.

Learning and Growth	
Insights:	**Tips:**
• People want to be part of a winning organization. • They want to make a difference. • They want to know you value them enough to invest in their learning and growth. • People want to learn and grow.	• Clarify what knowledge and skills your people need. • Ensure that every employee has a professional development plan. • Review their progress and success. • Provide feedback and support on a regular basis.

For information about available products and services visit www.businesspaths.net

Training and Development Needs Assessment

Department/Function/ Position	Knowledge/Skill/ Ability	Course Title	Description	Internal/ External	Delivered By:

Training and Development Needs Assessment - EXAMPLE

Department/Function/ Position	Knowledge/Skill/ Ability	Course Title	Description	Internal/ External	Delivered By:
First line manager	Communication	Your most important attribute	Focused on maximizing a variety of communication styles and techniques	external	Community College
	Conflict management	Say the Words	Learn how to facilitate conflict resolution; one-on-one and group approaches	internal	Community College
	Performance management & evaluation	Developing people to be the best they can be	How to set expectations, coach, provide meaningful feedback and assess ongoing performance	internal	Training
	Empowerment	Shared Power Works	Methods for engaging people and empowering them to make a difference	external	leadershipNOW LLC.
	Problem solving	Effective Problem Solving	Using a systematic approach to solving problems once and for all	external	leadershipNOW LLC
	Continuous improvement	Make a Difference – Innovation and Change	How to get everyone finding new and innovative ways to run the business	external	leadershipNOW LLC
	Team Development	A Guide to Self-Directed Teams	Learn how to create and develop self-directed teams	external	leadershipNOW LLC
	Leading change	Change that Matters	Effective methods for leading change while minimizing resistance	external	leadershipNOW LLC
	Meeting effectiveness	Meetings Worth Attending	How to plan and hold effective meetings	internal	Training
	Time management	The Care and Feeding of Monkeys	Help managers effectively invest their time in high pay-back activities	internal	Training
Administration					
Receptionist	Telephone System	Make the most of your system	Learn and maximize telephone system features	internal	Training
	Customer Service Skills	Build Customer Advocacy	Learn how to turn customers into raving fans	external	Community College

Commitment to Professional Development

Desired-State:

Prioritized Action(s)	Resource(s) Needed	Planned/Actual Completion	Comments/Status

Desired-State:

Prioritized Action(s)	Resource(s) Needed	Planned/Actual Completion	Comments/Status

Commitment to Professional Development – EXAMPLE

Desired-State: *Reduce my work week to 40 hours by investing my time more wisely*

Prioritized Action(s)	Resource(s) Needed	Planned/Actual Completion	Comments/Status
Participate in a time management class and develop actions that will support my goal.	Management approval	by the end of first quarter	
Plan and enter standing activities on my full-year calendar.	None	by the end of December	
Get people in the habit of bringing a recommended solution for every problem they bring to my attention.	None	Beginning January 1st, ongoing	

Desired-State:

Prioritized Action(s)	Resource(s) Needed	Planned/Actual Completion	Comments/Status

Team Development

_Together _everyone _achieves _more

In the world of rowing, attitude is more important than potential in building a winning team.

"Teamwork is the ability to work together toward a common vision. The ability to direct individual accomplishment toward organizational objectives. It is the fuel that allows common people to attain uncommon results

~Andrew Carnegie

Organizational flattening and the transition from autocratic to participative management styles have led to the creation and development of self-directed teams.

Rather than managers telling people what to do and how to do it, teams are told what needs to be accomplished and are then tasked with determining the best way to deliver the desired results. Many teams, whether functional, cross-functional, or virtual, are given the responsibility and authority for running their day-to-day business and are held accountable for their contributions to the success of their team and the organization as a whole. The synergy and collaboration gained through a team approach has a significant impact not only on performance, but also on employee morale, knowledge sharing, and reducing turnover.

Much more can be accomplished when members of teams pull together, share ideas, and solve problems, rather than when people work as individual contributors.

The benefits and challenges of teams:

Teams provide the most flexible and powerful work unit an organization can have. This is true when it comes to performance, learning, and change. That said, the creation and development of teams comes with its own set of benefits and challenges.

Potential Benefits:

- Higher levels of customer satisfaction
- Better understanding of the organization's mission
- Increased engagement and ownership
- Higher quality work at a lower cost
- Better communication
- Increased effectiveness and flexibility
- Greater employee development
- Higher levels of employee satisfaction

Potential Challenges:

- Managers style and roles may need to change
- Teams may resist taking on additional responsibility
- A great deal of training may be required
- Organizational systems may need to change
- Teams may take longer to make decisions
- Decisions may require more compromise
- A minority may dominate
- Fewer managers may be needed

The synergy and success of functional teams has led to the establishment of cross-functional teams, strategic partnerships, and with today's technology, virtual teams. When you bring people together and have them focus on common goals and tap into their knowledge and creativity, they will collectively find new and innovative ways to impact how work is done, solve problems, and deliver results. I've seen it throughout my years in leadership and consulting. There is nothing a team of people cannot do when they put their minds to it. And, with the challenges of today's business environment, organizations benefit greatly from the synergy.

How effective are your teams and partnerships?

One of the best ways to gauge where you are today and pinpoint areas that need focus and attention is to complete a self-assessment.

First, decide which group you will assess. The organization? A department? A team? Now, keep this group "top of mind," as you proceed through the self-assessment. Your ratings will identify conditions that contribute to team development and pinpoint areas that need additional focus and attention.

The Self-Assessment includes ten pairs of statements that represent factors that contribute to team development. Read the statement in the left-hand and right-hand column for each contributing factor. Place an "x" on the scale of one to seven that indicates where you view the team, department, or organization *today* in relationship to the two statements. If you find that part of the description rates higher and part lower, plot the lower rating on the scale of one to seven.

Here is an example of one pair of statements, and the rating scale:

CONTRIBUTING FACTOR:	WHERE WE ARE	WHERE WE NEED TO BE
Team Development: There is internal competition, individual contributor focus, and few joint efforts to improve how the team(s) operate.	X 1 2 3 4 5 6 7	**Team Development:** There is a spirit of cooperation that enables collaborative efforts to improve how the team(s) operate and how results are achieved.

If you decided to have other people participate in the self-assessment process, keep this in mind: People generally believe that their team or organization falls into a high-performing category. However, when I have facilitated the self-assessment process, I've noticed that, as groups review the summary of their individual ratings, they are astonished to find they've rated themselves extremely low. They even suggest that they must have been thinking about the organization when they applied the rating—certainly not their team.

When this situation became a barrier to moving forward with plans and actions to improve the team's effectiveness, I had them retake the self-assessment, being sure to focus on their team or group. In every situation, the overall ratings came out the same or lower than the original assessment.

The moral of the story:

- Ensure that everyone participating in the self-assessment is clear about which group he or she is assessing.
- Assure them that the overall assessment simply provides a starting point for developing plans and implementing actions that will increase the team or group's effectiveness.

If participants tell you, "It's tough settling on a rating," it's likely they feel that the group does well against some parts of the description and not so well against others. As a result, they have a tough time assigning a rating. Share the following example, which will help them feel more comfortable applying a rating.

> *As you read the statements in the left-hand and right-hand columns, let's say you believe that people generally cooperate with each other (a 6 rating), but there is regular competition and focus on individual contributions (a 2 rating). As a result, there is little focus on improving how teams operate (a 1 rating). You just came up with one 1, one 2, and one 6 rating.*

> *As you select an overall rating for this contributing Factor, "err on the low side" to ensure that areas receiving 1 and 2 ratings get addressed. In this example, you may choose to give Team Development an overall rating of 2.5*

Now, take a few minutes to complete the "power10" self-assessment on the following page for your organization or team.

Team Development Assessment for: _____

(i.e. ABC Company, Sales Department, Financial team)

Read the statements in the left-hand and right-hand columns for each of the ten Contributing Factors. Place an "x" on the scale of one to seven that indicates where you view the team, department, or organization *today* in relationship to the two statements.

CONTRIBUTING FACTOR	WHERE WE ARE	WHERE WE NEED TO BE
Team Development: There is internal competition, individual contributor focus, and few joint efforts to improve how the team(s) operate.	1 2 3 4 5 6 7	**Team Development:** There is a spirit of cooperation that enables collaborative efforts to improve how the team(s) operate and how results are achieved.
Commitment: There is not a sense of common purpose or shared ownership for achieving goals.	1 2 3 4 5 6 7	**Commitment:** Members are committed to the achievement of a common purpose and shared goals.
Communication: Communication is guarded, little sharing occurs, and conflicts go unresolved.	1 2 3 4 5 6 7	**Communication:** There is openness and honesty that allows members to share their views and openly confront and resolve conflicts.
Trust: There is little trust and limited cooperation amongst the members in achieving common goals.	1 2 3 4 5 6 7	**Trust:** There is a high level of mutual respect and trust that results in shared ownership and a commitment to common goals.
Roles and Responsibilities: Roles and responsibilities are unclear, causing confusion and a lack of accountability.	1 2 3 4 5 6 7	**Roles and Responsibilities:** Members have well-defined roles and a clear understanding of their responsibilities and accountability.
Diversity: Differing views and approaches are not well acknowledged or received by the majority of members.	1 2 3 4 5 6 7	**Diversity:** Members recognize and leverage the vast knowledge, skills, and experience that members bring to the team.
Empowerment: Decisions are made at management levels and shared with team members for implementation.	1 2 3 4 5 6 7	**Empowerment:** Members are given the responsibility, authority, and accountability for making decisions and solving problems that impact their day-to-day work.
Relationships: Little time and effort has been invested in building strong relationships that support team success.	1 2 3 4 5 6 7	**Relationships:** Strong working relationships have been established, which serve as the basis for achieving excellence.
Feedback: There is an absence of agreed-upon procedures for regular monitoring, reinforcement, and feedback.	1 2 3 4 5 6 7	**Feedback:** Members regularly monitor activities and provide feedback to reinforce the understanding and adherence to agreed-upon procedures.
Results: Performance is sporadic, which impacts member confidence and team morale.	1 2 3 4 5 6 7	**Results:** The team consistently delivers the desired results and members are recognized for their contributions and achievements.

Where does your organization or team need to focus?

To pinpoint which factors need work to develop effective teams, review your assessment and enter the three highest-rated and lowest-rated factors below.

Which three Contributing Factors did you rate the highest? (closest to seven)	Which three Contributing Factors did you rate the lowest? (closest to one)
1.	
2.	
3.	

Next Steps

- For those contributing factors rated the highest, keep doing what you are doing.
- For those contributing factors rated the lowest, take action to address them.

If you completed the self-assessment on your own and found value in the exercise, consider expanding the self-assessment to include other members of the organization or team. For example:

1. Have the Executive Team complete the self-assessment on the Executive Team.
2. Compile and summarize their ratings on a single, blank assessment sheet.
3. Utilize the assessment summary as the basis for discussion.
4. Delegate responsibility for developing plans and actions.
5. You may also choose to commission a task force to take charge of the planning process for a specific set of contributing factors.

Expanding involvement provides additional insights, commitment and support, which contributes to the effective development of teams throughout the organization.

If you have multiple teams or departments that you would like to participate in the self-assessment process, contact us at www.businesspaths.net to learn more about our on-line assessment services.

Essentials for successful teams

In the words of Margaret Mead, "Never doubt that a small group of thoughtful, committed people can change the world. Indeed. It is the only thing that ever has." However, to get all team members in the boat rowing the same direction, there are a number of essentials that contribute to the success of a team. They need to have:

- A common purpose
- Shared commitment

- Effective communication
- Support and trust
- Clear roles and responsibilities
- An appreciation for diversity
- Empowerment and accountability
- Strong relationships
- Regular and consistent feedback
- Consistent results

Building blocks for team development

In order to build strong teams, you need to ensure that they have an organizational understanding. Knowing what the organization stands for and believes in, where it is going and how it's going to get there provides a solid foundation, as teams plan how they will work together. Here is a set of building blocks for developing effective teams:

Building Blocks for Team Development

5. Agreed upon work processes

4. Performance goals and measures

3. Roles and responsibilities

2. Communication Plan

1. Code of Conduct

How the team will work together

4. Organizational priorities and focus

3. What the organization stands for and believes in

2. The fundamental reason for the organizations existence

1. What the future will look like

Organizational understanding

FOUNDATION

If there is an absence of information for you to provide on organizational understanding, you may find the chapter on "Common Purpose" helpful. Clearly, teams can navigate through the "How the team will work together" building blocks without these insights. However, when they have a line of sight to see how what they do and how their contributions support organizational success, the result is more effective.

Take Action—Call for a "power10"!

Get people working together

There are five building blocks for clarifying how team members will work together. The level of clarity that is achieved through the completion of these activities will have a significant impact on how effectively the team develops and performs. Let's take a closer look:

Create a Team Code of Conduct

The first step in clarifying how team members will work together is the development of a Code of Conduct.

Whether you prefer to call it a team charter or a code of conduct, members of the team establish guidelines for themselves that will result in a positive team climate. It calls for all team members to consistently model professional behaviors and take a consistent and healthy approach to achieving team success.

To establish a Code of Conduct, begin by having team members brainstorm responses to the following thought starters:

- What behaviors will support effective teamwork?
- How will we manage conflict?
- What do we need to do to build trust?
- How will we show dignity and respect for each other?
- What can we do to enhance communication?
- How do our customers expect us to act?
- What will it take to strengthen our relationships?
- What behaviors should we be modeling for our employees?
- How do we ensure that our meetings are meaningful and productive?
- What will support team and organizational success?

Once brainstorming is complete, you can have the team clarify and combine items with similar meanings and group them under common themes. Now, have the team review the Code of Conduct, make needed changes, and gain commitment to adhering to the code. You will find a work team and leadership team Code of Conduct example at the end of this chapter.

The Code of Conduct should be reviewed on a regular basis to reinforce adherence and commitment to what the team agreed to. In the event team members violate any part of team code, all members share responsibility for bringing the violation to the member's attention so they can again comply with the agreed-upon code.

Congratulations! The team has a behavioral framework to work within. Now, let's move on to how the team will communicate.

Establish a Communication Plan

Effective communication is the greatest challenge teams and organizations face. With communication being a major contributor to building relationships and trust, it is a critical element of teambuilding.

Teams need to clarify what information they need to be successful, determine how and when they will address a variety of situations, and how they will communicate. The development of a team Communication Plan serves as an invaluable tool in ensuring that the content and flow of information and communication occurs on a consistent basis.

Information on how to develop and implement a communication plan can be found in the chapter on *Communication*.

Clarify Roles and Responsibilities

During my years of consulting, one of the top three challenges for teams and organizations is clarifying people's roles and responsibilities. Without role clarity, you will generally find confusion and chaos… things falling through the cracks… people tripping over each other, as they attempt do the same things.

If your organization has Position Descriptions, chances are there is a section on essential roles and responsibilities. What I've found, however, is that where roles and responsibilities *are* defined, decision authority for the position is missing. If you find yourself in the position where you need to clarify roles and responsibilities, the following example should help.

First-line Manager Role	*Responsibilities*
What does the first-line manager routinely provide to his/her team and its members?	• Set clear direction. • Understand and ensure customer requirements are being met. • Communicate, inform, coach, provide feedback. • Empower and develop people to be the best they can be. • Model the behaviors outlined in organizational values. • Effectively manage the functional budget.
What additional responsibilities does a first-line manager have?	• Serve as an active member of the leadership team. • Collaborate cross-functionally to solve problems.

What operational decisions do first-line managers make?

- How their people are performing against expectations
- Where to spend money within budget guidelines
- Who to hire for their team

Congratulations! The team has clarified how it will work together, defined how and when it will communicate, and defined roles and responsibilities. Now, it's time to establish goals and clarify how you will gauge progress and success.

Set goals and establish metrics

What goals does your team(s) need to achieve in order to contribute to organizational success?

As each team delivers its "piece of the performance pie," organizational performance will be determined. Your responsibility is to ensure that the goals you establish and the means you put in place to measure progress and success are sound. The chapter on "Performance Management" will help you set goals and establish metrics.

Gain agreement on the team's work processes

One of the barriers to delivering consistent, predictable performance is an inconsistency of approach by team members. Though they believe everyone is being consistent, it is not necessarily the case. Why? The key work processes are not documented, so everyone has to rely on his or her own memory.

There are several advantages to clarifying and documenting work processes:

- Team members reach agreement on the work processes.
- When they are followed, work processes ensure a consist approach.
- Work processes are an excellent tool when orienting new team members.
- Consistent work processes provide a basis for continuous improvement efforts.

If team members are following the agreed upon processes and the team is delivering the required level of performance, the work processes are sound. If everyone is following the process and performance is not being achieved, the process needs to be modified, until it delivers needed performance.

The easiest way I've found for teams to document key work processes is to enter each step on a Post-It Note, then place them in an agreed-upon order on a large surface. This approach allows teams to move, add, or remove steps, until they reach agreement. Once complete, the process can be entered in a flowchart or displayed in a bulleted format.

Team development stages

As people come together to work in groups or as teams, they will transition through four stages of development. How long they remain in each stage will depend on their awareness of the stages and the actions they take to move to the next stage.

As the manager, your role will change, based on which stage the team is in, because their needs change as they move along the development continuum.

The Tuckman Model provides excellent insight into the stages of team development, outlined below:

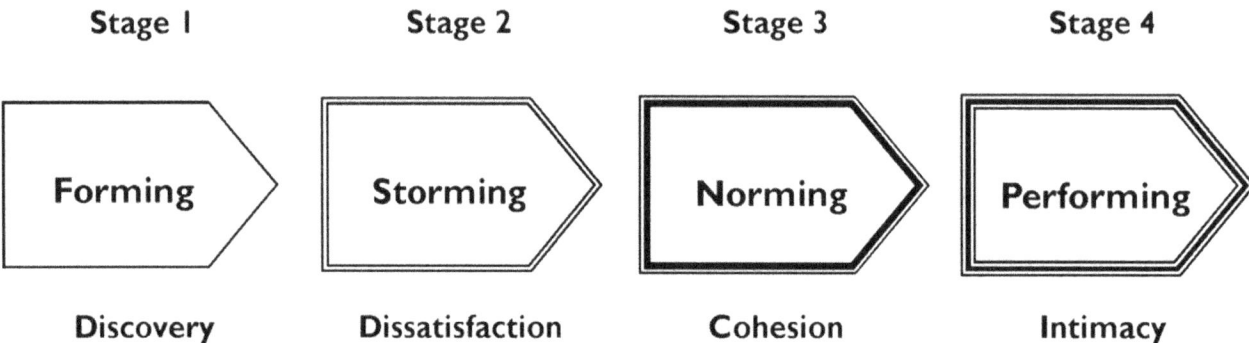

Stage 1	Stage 2	Stage 3	Stage 4
Forming	**Storming**	**Norming**	**Performing**
Discovery	Dissatisfaction	Cohesion	Intimacy

It would be wonderful if a team could be created and simply move through each stage only once. However, reality is a bit more complicated. As members of a team change, or new members are added, the team will go back to the "forming" stage and transition back through the stages again. They will most likely move through the stages faster than they did initially, because they have been building and developing the team, using the building-block approach covered earlier in this chapter.

The more turnover your teams have, the more time they will spend in the initial stages of development. The more stability your teams have, the more apt they are to reach and maintain the "performing" state, particularly if they used the building blocks to further team development.

What teams need from you changes. In the beginning they are much more dependent upon you for direction and support. As they develop they require less of your direct involvement.

How the manager's role changes as teams develop

Team members need different things from you as the team grows and develops. As a newly formed team, members will be much more dependent upon you as their manager. As they grow and develop, they will become more self-directed. Consequently, they need less and different things from you.

Let's take a look:

Forming	Storming	Norming	Performing
Team characteristics: Optimistic Positive expectations Anxiety and fear Guarded Dependent on leader	*Team characteristics:* Conflict Confusion & frustration Ineffectiveness Impatience Reduced productivity	*Team characteristics:* Accepting of team Increased trust and respect Sharing ideas and info. Two-way feedback Sense of team spirit	*Team characteristics:* Confident Working together Effective and efficient Strong performance Self challenging
Primary issues: Inclusion and trust The need to belong	*Primary issues:* Power and control Within the team	*Primary issues:* Leadership and control Team resolving conflict	*Primary issues:* Improving efficiency High performance
Leadership goal: Direct the team through the initial steps of team formation	*Leadership goal:* Increase the level of team interdependence	*Leadership goal:* Transition from content to facilitation and support; let go of control	*Leadership goal:* Remain engaged and supportive without regaining control
Focus: Role clarity *Style:* Directing *Decisions:* Command	*Focus:* Goals *Style:* Coaching *Decisions:* Consultative	*Focus:* Process *Style:* Facilitating *Decisions:* Collaborative	*Focus:* Relationships *Style:* Empowering *Decisions:* Consensus

Congratulations! You have the basis for building and developing teams, and insights into how your role changes to support a team's transition through their stages of development!

Team Development	
Insights:	**Tips:**
• Teams and partnerships make it easier to navigate ongoing challenges. • Teams can have a significant impact on performance, learning and change. • Managers' roles generally need to change. • Roles and responsibilities should include decision authority.	• Follow a building block approach to team development. • Understand how your management role changes as teams move through the development stages. • Stick with the process of developing teams and reap the rewards!

Leadership Team Code of Conduct – *EXAMPLE*

Teamwork/Performance

- Look at the big picture
- Focus on long-range planning vs. short-term fixes
- Be aware of organizational performance
- Be a team player
- Be a role model for our people
- Share ideas, knowledge, and experiences
- Be creative; take risks
- Be open to negotiation and change
- Don't tolerate gamesmanship
- Support peers in all situations
- Offer or seek help when needed
- Support the boss
- Reinforce our Code of Conduct

Trust/Caring

- Be more open and honest with each other
- Keep an open mind
- Care enough to communicate
- Talk to the person with whom you have a concern
- Trust each other
- Follow through on commitments
- Take time to know each other
- Give positive strokes
- Say "thank-you"
- Be sensitive to others' feelings
- It's okay to have fun

Communication/Respect

- Show respect for each other
- Be on time to all meetings
- Avoid gossiping inside or outside the organization
- Don't fly off the handle before getting the facts
- In conflict situations, go for win-win solutions
- Focus on the issues not personalities
- Give constructive feedback
- It is okay to disagree, but "no" should be the last alternative
- Support the "family" unit

Work Team Code of Conduct – *EXAMPLE*

AS MEMBERS OF THE TEAM WE WILL:

Operate as a team, by:

- Bringing our best selves to work
- Ensuring that everyone feels welcome
- Working as a team toward group and individual goals
- Asking for support when we need it

Show respect for one another, by:

- Showing unconditional respect
- Assuming good intentions
- Taking issues we have to the person
- Honoring each other's authentic experience
- Being forgiving when mistakes are made

Communicate effectively, by:

- Communicating honestly, openly, and clearly
- Listening to understand, not just to respond
- Allowing others to speak without interruption
- Asking for clarification when we do not understand
- Giving and receiving honest feedback
- Speaking with appropriate tone and volume
- Implementing a respectful way to share frustrations

Hold effective meetings, by:

- Determining the purpose prior to scheduling
- Publishing an agenda in advance of the meeting
- Distributing handouts, timelines, etc., in advance of the meeting
- Showing up! Being present physically and mentally
- Coming prepared to meetings
- Speaking for ourselves; owning our own ideas, beliefs, feelings
- Focusing on the "big picture"
- Avoiding sidebars
- Debating the issues; agreeing to disagree
- Giving people a chance to think. Silence is okay
- Creating clear actions
- Taking responsibility for missed meetings
- Ending meetings on a positive note

Make sound decisions, by:

- Determining if we are a decision-making body or advising body before accepting or designing projects
- Making fact-based decisions
- Ensuring that the right people are involved in decisions
- Engaging in problem solving

Environment

Become an employer of choice

Winning rowing teams emerge from an environment where everyone performs his or her best and pulls as hard as he or she can. Crewmembers are at the starting line on time; they execute their plan, steer well, and maintain a safe environment for the team. What environment have you created for the people who work for and with you?

Organizational cultures and work environments are interesting studies. Try walking into a variety of organizations and see what your initial perception is. Imagine for a moment what it would be like to work there:

- How it would it feel to get up and report to work there every day?
- What's your sense about the products and services the organization offers?
- How satisfied do you think their customers might be?
- What level of success do you imagine the organization is having?

Some initial impressions will find you wanting to turn around and leave as quickly as you arrived.

What messages does your work environment send? Are people knocking down your door to come to work for you? Do your employees take pride in the success of the organization? What kind of work environment do your people get up and come to work in every day? Let's take a look at some contrasting conditions:

Do you have an environment where:	Or:
Everyone strives for excellence.	People work to maintain the status quo.
There is a common sense of purpose.	People work in functional silos.
Pro-active approaches are sought.	People react to situations and conditions.
Open, honest communication is the norm.	Communication is limited and inconsistent.
Relationships and trust are built.	Suppression and suspicion prevail.
People are considered the most valuable asset.	People are considered expendable.

Professional development is ongoing.	Training and development are not a priority.
People know how they contribute to organizational success.	People are unaware of strategies and goals.
Inclusion and empowerment are part of the environment.	People are told what to do and how to do it.
Teamwork and collaboration are standard.	Focus is on individual contributions.
Win-win outcomes are the norm.	Win-lose outcomes tend to prevail.
There is accountability for actions and performance.	People have a sense of entitlement.
Results are consistently achieved.	Performance is sporadic.
People are recognized for their contributions.	There is little reward and recognition.

Eighty percent of performance improvement opportunities are located in the environment.

Price Pritchet, *Managing Sideways*

Your most valuable assets for meeting the challenges of today's changing business environment are the people that work with and for you. Unfortunately, over the decades, many organizations have fallen prey to bottom-line focus and short-term decision making. They have lost sight of the fact that their most valuable asset is their people, and that it is through them that their teams and organization will be successful.

What happens in reality?

Participants in a Sirota Survey Intelligence study that spanned a three-year period and included 3.5 million staff members indicated that their managers, far from driving the business forward, actually hamper progress. The study also revealed the following insights:

Three basic workers' desires are to:

1. Know what is expected of them
2. Have competent bosses, and
3. Have better cooperation across the firm

They identified the biggest challenge for companies: creating an enthusiastic workforce.

How does your team or organization stack up?

These results are fairly common. You will find many studies with similar findings across the country and around the world. The breadth of information gleaned from these surveys suggests that managers and leaders have some work to do to create an environment that attracts and retains the best and brightest to carry the organization successfully into the future.

So, as you think about your current environment, it's important to remember that people want to be part of a winning organization, where they know they can make a difference. It is important that they know what they are a part of, where the organization is headed, how it's going to get there, and where they fit in. They want to know what's expected, how they are doing, and feel confident that they can contribute to overall success. In addition, they want to be treated with dignity and respect, have the opportunity to learn and grow, and feel that their contributions are valued and recognized.

In your leadership role, you need to set the pace and tone for your organization, department, or team. How effectively you model the values and guiding principles of the organization, follow accepted practices, and adhere to established policies will have a significant impact on the overall environment. One of your most important roles is that of communicator. Whether you are talking with a customer, negotiating with a supplier, or working with your people, your ability to gain trust and build sound relationships is paramount to an open, honest work environment.

When you bring your people together, focus them on common goals, and tap into their knowledge and creativity, they will collectively find new and innovative ways to impact how work is done, solve problems, and deliver performance.

How healthy is your organization's environment?

Take a few minutes to complete the following self-assessment.

First, decide which group you will assess. The organization? A department? A team? Now, keep this group "top of mind," as you proceed through the self-assessment. Your ratings will identify conditions that contribute to a healthy environment, and pinpoint areas that need additional focus and attention.

The Self-Assessment includes ten pairs of statements that represent factors that contribute to a healthy environment. Read the statement in the left-hand and right-hand column for each contributing factor. Place an "x" on the scale of one to seven that indicates where you view the team, department, or organization *today* in relationship to the two statements. If you find that part of the description rates higher and part lower, plot the lower rating on the scale of one to seven.

Here is an example of one pair of statements, and the rating scale:

CONTRIBUTING FACTOR	WHERE WE ARE	WHERE WE NEED TO BE
Environment: There is little trust established, which results in conflict and win-lose outcomes	 1 2 3 4 5 6 7	**Environment:** There is a high level of trust and mutual respect that allows members to feel valued for their contributions, and win-win outcomes to be achieved

If you decided to have other people participate in the self-assessment process, keep this in mind: People generally believe that their team or organization falls into a high-performing category. However, when I have facilitated the self-assessment process, I've noticed that, as groups review the summary of their individual ratings, they are astonished to find they've rated themselves extremely low. They even suggest that they must have been thinking about the organization when they applied the rating—certainly not their team.

When this situation became a barrier to moving forward with plans and actions to improve the team's effectiveness, I had them retake the self-assessment, being sure to focus on their team or group. In every situation, the overall ratings came out the same or lower than the original assessment.

The moral of the story:

- Ensure that everyone participating in the self-assessment is clear about which group he or she is assessing.

- Assure them that the overall assessment simply provides a starting point for developing plans and implementing actions that will increase the team or group's effectiveness.

If participants tell you, "It's tough settling on a rating," it's likely they feel that the group does well against some parts of the description and not so well against others. As a result, they have a tough time assigning a rating. Share the following example, which will help them feel more comfortable applying a rating.

As you read the statements in the left-hand and right-hand columns, let's say you believe that trust poses a significant issue (a 1 rating), but people are treated reasonably well (a 3 rating). Members feel valued, but are not formally recognized for their contributions (a 4 rating). Win-lose outcomes tend to be the norm (a 2 rating). You just came up with one 1, one 2, one 3, and one 4 rating.

As you select an overall rating for this contributing Factor, "err on the low side" to ensure that areas receiving 1 and 2 ratings get addressed. In this example, you may choose to give Environment an overall rating of 2.0

Now, take a few minutes to complete the "power10" self-assessment on the following page for your organization or team.

Environment Assessment for: _____

(i.e. ABC Company, Sales Department, Finance Team)

Read the statements in the left-hand and right-hand columns for each of the ten Contributing Factors. Place an "x" on the scale of one to seven that indicates where you view the team, department, or organization *today* in relationship to the two statements.

CONTRIBUTING FACTOR	WHERE WE ARE	WHERE WE NEED TO BE
Environment: There is little trust established, which results in conflict and win-lose outcomes.	1 2 3 4 5 6 7	**Environment:** There is a high level of trust and mutual respect that allows members to feel valued for their contributions and win-win outcomes to be achieved.
People: There is little importance placed on the people asset; members are viewed as expendable resources that can be replaced.	1 2 3 4 5 6 7	**People:** Members are viewed as a valuable asset in running and managing a successful team, department, or organization.
Leadership: There is a low regard for management, contributing to an "us and them" attitude, internal competition, and less than desired performance.	1 2 3 4 5 6 7	**Leadership:** Members respect management's involvement and commitment to making a better place to work, as well as successfully delivering results.
Collaboration: Members seldom work together to address problems or collectively improve how the overall work is done.	1 2 3 4 5 6 7	**Collaboration:** There is a cooperative team approach to addressing problems and collectively improving how the work is done.
Learning and Growth: Members are protective of individual knowledge and are reluctant to share their expertise with others.	1 2 3 4 5 6 7	**Learning and Growth:** There is a strong commitment to continuous learning and knowledge-sharing to enhance individual and overall effectiveness.
Communication: Communication is guarded, which limits trust and inhibits working together to get the job done.	1 2 3 4 5 6 7	**Communication:** There is an environment of openness and honesty at all levels that fosters trust and commitment to getting the job done.
Consistency: There is a lack of consistency in how members are managed and how the work is approached.	1 2 3 4 5 6 7	**Consistency:** Managers regularly model the values and uphold the overriding philosophy and principles while leading the team, department or organization.
Fairness and Equitability: There are inconsistencies in how members are treated and how practices are applied, causing the perception of favoritism.	1 2 3 4 5 6 7	**Fairness and Equitability:** Consistently applied practices ensure that members receive fair and equitable treatment.
Excellence: Members are comfortable with maintaining the status quo, rather than breaking away from the way things have always been done.	1 2 3 4 5 6 7	**Excellence:** There is a strong commitment to finding new and innovative ways to deliver quality products and services and improve how the work is done.
Confidence: There is little confidence in leadership and overall direction, causing low morale, instability, and turnover.	1 2 3 4 5 6 7	**Confidence:** There is a high degree of confidence in the future, leadership and overall direction.

Where does your organization or team need to focus?

To pinpoint which factors need work to create and maintain a healthy environment, review your assessment and enter the three highest-rated and lowest-rated factors below.

Which three Contributing Factors did you rate the highest? (closest to seven)	Which three Contributing Factors did you rate the lowest? (closest to one)
1.	
2.	
3.	

Next Steps

- For those contributing factors rated the highest, keep doing what you are doing.
- For those contributing factors rated the lowest, take action to address them.

If you completed the self-assessment on your own and found value in the exercise, consider expanding the self-assessment to include other members of the organization or team. For example:

1. Have the Executive Team complete the self-assessment on the organization.
2. Compile and summarize their ratings on a single, blank assessment sheet.
3. Utilize the assessment summary as the basis for discussion.
4. Delegate responsibility for developing plans and actions to existing teams or standing committees.
5. You may also choose to commission a task force to take charge of the planning process for a specific set of contributing factors.

Expanding involvement provides additional insights, commitment, and support, which contributes to creating and maintaining a healthy work environment.

If you have multiple teams or departments that you would like to participate in the self-assessment process, contact us at www.businesspaths.net to learn more about our on-line assessment services.

What does it take to attract and retain the right people?

There are lessons to be learned from the ten companies named 2010's best companies to work for. SAS provides daycare on campus, Edward Jones allows people to customize their business approach, and Wegmans Food Markets offers opportunities for career advancement, to name a few. And yes, they provide some perks that most companies are not in a position to offer. However, there are common themes across these organizations that do not require hard dollars…they are investments that reflect the value and care the organization has for its people.

The most prevalent theme includes a "family" type environment. When people get to know each other as people and learn about each other's families, they build relationships, trust, and a strong sense of community. This results in a very supportive environment, where people collaborate and work together to achieve success. In addition, they feel valued and they appreciate having the opportunity for professional development and growth.

Ordinary people can achieve extraordinary things when they get to know each other, when their managers understand what each employee's unique needs are, and when people work together to deliver team and organizational goals.

Have you been part of an environment similar to what I just described?

Reflect on a time when you thoroughly enjoyed getting up and heading for work. You loved your job and enjoyed working with a dedicated group of people who were highly successful.

What did you enjoy the most about the environment? About your job? What set the organization apart from the others you have worked for? Enter your thoughts below.

The environment	Your job	The organization

How many of these characteristics exist in your environment today? Which ones need work? And which additional environmental factors need to be developed?

Why people quit their jobs

According to a Gallup poll of more than one million employed U. S. Workers, a bad boss or supervisor is the number one reason people quit their jobs. Survey findings also state that poorly managed work groups are on average 50 percent less productive and 44 percent less profitable than well-managed groups.

Other reasons cited in surveys why people quit their jobs:

- Under-staffing
- Poor communication
- Lack of challenge
- Lack of empowerment
- No recognition
- Unclear direction and priorities
- Questionable promotion practices
- Limited flexibility for life situations

People don't quit their jobs, they quit their managers

Though it may be easy to be lulled into thinking that pay is the main contributor, not one of these reasons deals with pay, and they all can be controlled by those in management. Turnover not only disrupts the team or organization, it has a negative impact on customer confidence. And then, there is the financial impact—it costs upwards of one and one-half times a person's salary to replace them.

What level of turnover does your organization experience?

Take Action—Call for a "power10"!

Build relationships and trust

Stephen M.R. Covey in his book, *The Speed of Trust*, shares the following statistics on organizational trust within companies:

- 51 percent of employees have trust and confidence in Senior Management.
- 36 percent of employees believe their leaders act with honesty and integrity.
- Over the past twelve months, 76 percent of employees observed illegal or unethical conduct on the job that, if exposed, could seriously violate public trust.

How would your people respond?

The *Speed of Trust* is the best book I've read on building organizational trust. Covey shares that demonstrating both character and competence provide the right balance for gaining trust. And he points out that integrity, motive, and intent are the basis for character, and capabilities, skills, results, and track record reflect one's competence.

Why is trust so darned important? Because organizations where there is high trust perform three times better than organizations plagued with low trust. They also have a strong work environment and a competitive advantage.

On the relationship front, how much do you know about your people, their families, and what they need? How about the name of the family pet? If you find your list is short, build a profile on each of your people and refer to it often. Then, inquire periodically, using specific family or pet names. When you approach your people in a casual and sincere manner, they will know that you value them, and care about their family as an important part of their life.

Communication is the key to building relationships and trust.
And trust is the glue that holds it all together.

The days of treating employees like a number, or a commodity to be discarded, are over. The old ways simply do not work anymore! People not only expect more from their managers, they deserve to be treated with dignity and respect. They are your most valuable resource as you move the team or organization into the future.

Reshape your culture and environment

People spend half their waking hours at work, and half alone, with family or friends, involved in a variety of activities. If you want to get the most out of your people and be viewed as an employer of choice, employees' time at work needs to be meaningful, productive, and rewarding.

The culture and environment of an organization is comprised of a variety of factors and have profound influence on how people feel, perform, and behave. They include organizational legends, shared attitudes, values and goals, supervisory and management practices, and stakeholder relationships, to name a few. So, when you set out to reshape your culture or environment, it will take time, commitment, and continued focus. Depending upon the size of your organization and the consistency of focus, it can take several years to reach the desired culture and environment.

To have a positive impact on the work environment, managers and leaders need to ensure that:

- Satisfying customers is an organizational priority whether you deliver products or provide services.

- They set the pace and tone for their people.
- People are recognized as your most valuable asset.
- Employees feel valued and respected for who they are and what they do.
- Everyone is treated fairly and equitably.
- They take responsibility for developing their people to be the best they can be.
- They engage their people in running the day-to-day business.
- They know when problems surface in the organization or on a team…it is a leadership issue.
- Managers and leaders are comfortable "saying the words."
- They are proactive and forward thinking in their approach.
- They manage things and lead people!
- They get everyone in the boat rowing the same direction.

Environment	
Insights:	**Tips:**
<ul><li>It takes time and commitment to change a culture or environment.</li><li>High-trust organizations perform three times better than low-trust organizations.</li><li>Consistency is key to building relationships and trust.</li><li>Only slightly more than one third of employees believe their leaders act with honesty and integrity.</li></ul>	<ul><li>Leadership behaviors have a significant impact on the work environment.</li><li>Effective communication is key to building relationships and trust.</li><li>People quit their manager, not their job.</li><li>Show an interest in your employees and their needs.</li><li>Morale is better in organizations that perform well.</li></ul>

For information about available products and services visit www.businesspaths.net

Results

Pull ahead of the competition and cross the finish line!

Were you hired to get results? Of course you were. Just as the Coxswain steers the boat and motivates the crew to deliver their best rowing performance, your position exists to set the direction and organize resources in a way that delivers results. Though this may sound simple, in reality, results reflect the culmination of what you have built as the leader of your team or organization. Achieving consistent, predictable results takes getting everyone in the boat rowing the same direction to cross the finish line and end up on the medal stand.

Common barriers to delivering results include ineffective communication, a lack of engagement and accountability, and an absence of planning and execution.

About 70 percent of organizational failures are due to poor execution

Contributing factors include: no clarity, no commitment, no line of sight, no empowerment, no synergy, no accountability

---

Franklin Covey Developing x! Execution Intelligence
Survey of 12,000 people

As a leader, you play a critical role in your team or organization's success. Your role involves setting clear direction, deploying that direction and having a performance management process in place to ensure achievement and over-achievement of the desired results. If you believe you've set the direction and you've got your resources organized and focused, the question becomes: *How will you know when your team or organization delivers the desired level of performance and is positioned to compete in today and tomorrow's environment?*

During my years of consulting, I've seen managers become a barrier to delivering performance. In addition to unclear direction and a lack of engagement, a lot of great ideas and plans got set aside because they were not fully developed and implemented. Let's take a look at how you can ensure that you get everyone in the boat rowing in the same direction to deliver the results you need.

What results does your crew need to deliver?

First, clarify what constitutes success for your team or organization. Just as most people would not embark on a journey without a destination in mind, you need to know what success looks like for your area of responsibility. How will you know that your team or organization is delivering the level of results necessary to pull ahead of the competition and cross the finish line?

Organizations focused on delivering balanced performance generally pursue results in four major categories:

1. Providing customer value
2. Delivering financial results
3. Utilizing effective processes and systems
4. Growing and developing people

Take a few minutes to list how you measure your team or organization's success:

Customer Value:	Financial Results:
i.e., growing market share, attracting new business, retaining existing business, building customer loyalty, etc.	i.e., maximizing ROI, increasing profitability, growing revenue, reducing costs, etc.
▪	▪
▪	▪
▪	▪
▪	▪
Processes and Systems:	**People Growth & Development:**
i.e., delivering quality products and services, responding to customer and business requirements, implementing innovative improvements, etc.	i.e., hiring and retaining quality personnel, expanding knowledge and skills, effectively utilizing technology, etc.
▪	▪
▪	▪
▪	▪
▪	▪

If it was fairly easy to complete this exercise, congratulations. You're most likely headed in the right direction. If completing it posed a few challenges, it's important to ensure that the organization has goals and objectives that the departments and teams align themselves based on the role they play in organizational success. How does your list measure up?

Unique characteristics of high-performing organizations

As we explore how your role supports the achievement of results, let's take a look at the unique characteristics of high-performing organizations.

You will find that consistently high-performing organizations are intensely focused on their customers. They strive to understand and consistently meet or exceed changing external customer requirements. And they consider their people their internal customers, and most valuable assets.

These organizations create a common sense of purpose that all employees share and actively engage their people in continually improving how the work is done and how results are achieved. People understand the organization's destination, participate in determining how to get there, and receive recognition for their contributions to overall success. As a result, employees focus a collective effort on growing and developing the business and achieving desired results.

High-performing organizations establish stretch goals. They have a means for tracking progress and success, and use management information to make fact-based, informed decisions to address business and performance issues. Their people know what level of performance to strive for and what contributions they are making on an ongoing basis.

These organizations have created an environment where employees feel valued, are held accountable to delivering results, and receive recognition for their contributions to the success of the organization, department, and team.

The criticality of your role

Significant demands on both time and resources pose many challenges for people in management positions. These demands, coupled with financial tightening, finds leaders searching for ways to do more with less, while ensuring that their people deliver the needed results. Consequently, leaders must consistently focus on the pivotal role they play in delivering sustainable results.

In your leadership role you need to:

- Set the pace and tone—set clear direction, align your people behind the direction and implement an overall performance management process.
- Actively engage your people in planning and implementation—to drive ownership and gain commitment.

- Motivate your people—provide ongoing coaching and feedback and intervene when the boat veers off course.
- Hold people accountable for delivering needed results.
- Ensure that your people feel valued—recognize their contributions to overall success.

How effectively does your team or organization deliver consistent, predictable results?

Take a few minutes to complete the following self-assessment.

First, decide which group you will assess. The organization? A department? A team? Now, keep this group "top of mind," as you proceed through the self-assessment. Your ratings will identify conditions that contribute to getting consistent results and pinpoint areas that need additional focus and attention.

The Self-Assessment includes ten pairs of statements that represent factors that contribute to getting consistent results. Read the statement in the left-hand and right-hand column for each contributing factor. Place an "x" on the scale of one to seven that indicates where you view the team, department, or organization *today* in relationship to the two statements. If you find that part of the description rates higher and part lower, plot the lower rating on the scale of one to seven.

Here is an example of one pair of statements and the rating scale:

CRITICAL SUCCESS FACTOR:	WHERE WE ARE	WHERE WE NEED TO BE
Results: Performance results are sporadic, which negatively impacts member confidence and morals.	X 1 2 3 4 5 6 7	**Results:** Desired results are consistently delivered, with members being recognized for their contributions and achievements.

If you decided to have other people participate in the self-assessment process, keep this in mind: People generally believe that their team or organization falls into a high-performing category. However, when I have facilitated the self-assessment process, I've noticed that, as groups review the summary of their individual ratings, they are astonished to find they've rated themselves extremely low. They even suggest that they must have been thinking about the organization when they applied the rating—certainly not their team.

When this situation became a barrier to moving forward with plans and actions to improve the team's effectiveness, I had them retake the self-assessment, being sure to focus on their team or group. In every situation, the overall ratings came out the same or lower than the original assessment.

The moral of the story:

- Ensure that everyone participating in the self-assessment is clear about which group he or she is assessing.

- Assure them that the overall assessment simply provides a starting point for developing plans and implementing actions that will increase the team or group's effectiveness.

If participants tell you, "It's tough settling on a rating," it's likely they feel that the group des well against some parts of the description and not so well against others. As a result, they have a tough time assigning a rating. Share the following example, which will help them feel more comfortable applying a rating.

As you read the statements in the left-hand and right-hand columns, let's say you believe that results are sporadic (a 3 rating), but people are recognized for their contributions (a 6 rating). People are concerned about the future of the organization and their job (a 1 rating). You just came up with one 1, one 3, and one 6 rating.

As you select an overall rating for this contributing factor, "err on the low side" to ensure that areas receiving 1 and 3 ratings get addressed. In this example, you may choose to give Results an overall rating of 2.0

Now, take a few minutes to complete the "power10" self-assessment on the following page for your organization or team.

Results Assessment for: _____

(i.e. ABC Company, Sales Department, Finance Team)

Read the statements in the left-hand and right-hand columns for each of the ten (10) Contributing Factors. Place an "x" on the scale of 1 – 7 that indicates where you view the team, department, or organization *today* in relationship to the two statements.

CONTRIBUTING FACTOR	WHERE WE ARE	WHERE WE NEED TO BE
Results: Performance results are sporadic, which negatively impacts member confidence and morale.	1 2 3 4 5 6 7	**Results:** Desired results are consistently delivered, with members being recognized for their contributions and achievements.
Customer Loyalty: There is a lack of information or understanding of customer requirements or ways to add customer value.	1 2 3 4 5 6 7	**Customer Loyalty:** Members understand and consistently meet customer requirements and continually seek ways to add customer value.
Financial Performance: There is a lag in reporting financial performance, which places teams, departments, and the organization at risk of consistent financial achievement.	1 2 3 4 5 6 7	**Financial Performance:** There is a consistent level of awareness and visibility brought to spending levels and revenue generation.
Employee Satisfaction: There are insufficient methods for assessing member satisfaction or understanding the contributors to turnover.	1 2 3 4 5 6 7	**Employee Satisfaction:** There is an ongoing process for understanding the levels of employee satisfaction and for taking actions to affect improvement.
Management Information: Information to make decisions and manage the team, department, or organization is not readily available or produced in a usable format.	1 2 3 4 5 6 7	**Management Information:** There is a comprehensive MIS that accurately reflects current performance trends and ongoing results.
Tracking and Monitoring: Efforts to track progress and monitor performance are ineffective or non-existent, resulting in a lack of accountability.	1 2 3 4 5 6 7	**Tracking and Monitoring:** Effective methods for tracking progress and monitoring results are in place. Which are regularly utilized as the basis for accountability.
Key Measures: There are not established measures to reflect performance against common goals.	1 2 3 4 5 6 7	**Key Measures:** There are established measures that reflect performance against a critical few set of metrics.
Progress Measures: There is an absence of indicators to show progress against achieving the desired results.	1 2 3 4 5 6 7	**Progress Measures:** There are established measures that reflect progress being made against achieving the desired results.
Performance Reviews: There are inconsistencies in how performance is reviewed or little understanding of where focus and improvements are needed.	1 2 3 4 5 6 7	**Performance Reviews:** Performance is reviewed on a regular basis to celebrate successes and identify areas for continued focus and improvement.
Reward and Recognition: There is not an effective plan in place to reward individual and team contributions.	1 2 3 4 5 6 7	**Reward and Recognition:** Formal and informal recognition plans are in place to provide individual and team reward and recognition.

Where does your organization or team need to focus?

To pinpoint which factors need work to support the achievement of your desired results, review your assessment and enter the three highest-rated and lowest-rated factors below.

Which three Contributing Factors did you rate the highest? (closest to seven)	Which three Contributing Factors did you rate the lowest? (closest to one)
1.	
2.	
3.	

Next Steps

- For those contributing factors rated the highest, keep doing what you are doing
- For those contributing factors rated the lowest, take action to address them

If you have multiple teams or departments that you would like to participate in the self-assessment process, contact us at www.businesspaths.net to learn more about our on-line assessment services.

How to get results

If you want your team or organization to deliver consistent, predictable results, it begins with you setting the pace and tone for your people. You need to set clear direction and recognize that the expectations you establish and uphold will determine the level of performance your team or organization will achieve.

The role you play will make the difference between your people delivering mediocre, good, or outstanding performance.

Take Action—Call for a "power10"!

Set clear direction

Whether you choose to work independently or actively involve the people who work for you in developing direction, setting clear direction provides the opportunity to paint a picture of the future (a vision) for your team or organization and clarify the fundamental reason for its existence (the purpose). In addition, you need to clarify and uphold the organizational values and behaviors you expect from both your people and those with whom they work.

With that foundation built, you can clarify the critical few priorities you want your team or organization to focus on. This process includes establishing goals and objectives for each priority and includes a timeframe for achieving them. Some goals and objectives will have quantifiable results, while others will be measured, as milestones are accomplished along the way. The goals you set should be stretch goals. They should reflect the minimum level of performance you will accept and include the metrics that will be used for gauging progress and measuring success.

Once you have completed these steps, you have essentially created a Vision, Mission, and Values and established priorities, goals, and objectives. When you add their respective metrics, you will have a method for gauging the progress and success of your team or organization. If you need additional help setting clear direction, refer to the chapter on "Common Purpose" for additional information, tips, and tools.

Your next step…deploying direction.

Align your team or organization behind the direction

With the direction set, it's time to communicate it to all members of your team or organization. Whether you have responsibility for leading ten people, one hundred employees, or an organization of one thousand, having everyone in the boat rowing the same direction will move the boat swiftly toward the finish line. In order to maximize the effectiveness of the crew and usher the boat across the finish line, your people need to understand where they fit in the overall picture and have a clear line-of-sight for how their contributions support overall success. If 100 percent of your people are not engaged, it will be like some employees are sitting on barges causing a drag on the boat, which places winning the race at risk.

Departments and teams play different roles in the organization. As a result, their goals, plans, and actions need to reflect the role they play in support of organizational achievement. Once people understand the destination of the organization, how it plans to get there, and how it will measure success, they can develop their plans and actions. Their plans should include who is responsible for coordinating implementation of the plans and actions within the expected due dates. You will find a blank action document for their use on page 45.

Once you have the teams aligned with organizational direction, it's time to establish individual performance expectations. You will have successfully cascaded direction throughout the organization and have departments, teams, and individuals in the boat, once the individual expectations have been established.

The development and implementation of individual plans and actions will get everyone rowing in the same direction. And, when you implement your performance management process, you can steer the boat and motivate your crew through the use of coaching, feedback, and recognition for a job well done.

Now you are ready to manage the direction.

Implement a performance management process

With direction communicated, departments, teams, and individuals having developed and implemented their plans and actions with metrics in place to gauge progress and measure success...What's next? One of the most important parts of the entire process is inspecting what you expect. This critical activity frequently gets overlooked, until it's too late to positively impact performance and results! You need to be prepared to intervene *before* the boat has gone off course.

In the chapter on Performance Management, you were introduced to a Key Indicator Trend Report. It serves as a vital tool in bringing visibility to how the team or organization is performing in key areas of the business. When you can see how the organization is performing every month, significant shifts or trends that could threaten delivering the desired results can be explored and actions planned and taken before it is too late to impact quarterly or annual performance. It is an excellent tool to support fact-based decision-making and can be used as the basis for conducting regular performance reviews.

Throughout the direction-setting process, responsibility for coordinating and overseeing the implementation of agreed-upon actions were assigned to individuals. So, it's time to pull those people together on a regular basis and ask them to provide a status on implementation of the plans and actions. You may choose to have them come together as departments or ask representatives from the entire organization to come together all at once, depending on the size and number of representatives you have assigned coordination and oversight responsibility.

This forum provides the opportunity for the assigned representatives to share the progress that their respective groups have made and lets you know if the plans and actions are on track. If not, you need to intervene to help get them back on track. When you have peers participate in these forums, it adds an incentive to keep everyone on top of their responsibilities and headed toward the finish line.

Initially, I would recommend holding status sessions on a monthly basis to ensure that teams and departments get off to a strong start, as the race gets underway. This frequency gives you the opportunity to intervene early in the process if needed. And as you gain confidence that the coordinators are maintaining focus and driving continued progress, you may choose to adjust the frequency of the status sessions. Just make sure that whatever frequency you choose maintains a frequency that allows time for intervention and recovery should the boat veer off course.

Hold people accountable

Over the past several decades, organizations found themselves in an "era of entitlement," versus one of accountability. There has even been a debate about whether people take accountability or if they should be held accountable.

My years of consulting have uncovered a lack of direction and expectations and the absence of a means for gauging progress and success. The following survey results from a Developing x! Execution Intelligence survey of 12,000 people conducted by Franklin Covey in 2003 found that only:

> ### Half of all workers report that they:
> - **Feel accountable for goal performance**
> - **Are rarely if ever called upon to report progress**
> - **Feel any responsibility to meet budgetary commitments**

If only half of the people feel this way, what do the rest of them think and believe?

As I've asked CEOs and leadership teams, "*How do you know when you hand out the pay checks that you're getting the return on your labor dollar investment that you need?*" I've gotten many blank stares and few responses. The truth of the matter is that some organizations have no system for setting expectations or consistently addressing performance issues. Some have no formal recognition plans, while others pay bonuses to their employees just because they think they should.

It's important to remember:

> ### "What gets measured becomes important!" and "If we can't measure it, we can't control it.
> ### If we can't control it, we can't manage it."

Throughout *"power10" Leadership*, I have emphasized the importance of establishing goals, setting expectations, and having metrics to gauge the progress and success of individuals, teams, departments, and the organization. Without these key elements, you simply leave arrival at your destination to chance.

In today's competitive environment, your people need to know that you are serious about delivering results. They need to understand that you pay them to be active participants and contributors to the success of the team and organization. And they need to know that holding up their end of the bargain is a condition of employment.

Having a Performance Management Process provides the basis for accountability throughout the organization.

Recognize people's contributions

Recognition should be used to reinforce professional behaviors that support overall success and recognize employees, teams, and departments for their contributions. A highly valued, often overlooked and underutilized form of recognition is simply...catching people in the act of doing things right and saying, "Thank you for a job well done."

"What gets recognized gets done and what gets rewarded gets repeated."

Michael LeBonef

As you look at your existing recognition program, does it accomplish what you need it to, or do you need to develop a new one? Consider the following:

- What philosophy does your organization have surrounding reward and recognition?
- Does your current reward and recognition program positively impact performance, behavior, the culture?
- What behaviors do you need throughout the team/organization to be successful?
- How can you utilize reward and recognition to help change the team/ organization in profound ways?
- What forms of recognition do your people believe express the greatest appreciation and have the most meaning?
- What budget has been allocated for recognition?

With these thoughts in mind, decide what combination of incentive and discretionary recognition you will implement in addition to regularly finding people in the act of doing things right...the most meaningful form of recognition.

Develop a recognition plan

Let's talk about how you will approach the plan development. Will you build the plan independently or pull together a representative group of employees to help develop it?

Second, decide what form(s) of recognition will be included in the plan:

Form of recognition:	What it's used for:	Here's an example:
Incentive Recognition	• Pre-determined levels of performance that must be met to receive recognition. • Communicated and understood at the beginning of the recognition period.	• Delivering 115% of sales plan for the quarter • Zero customer complaints on a monthly basis • Increased production by 5%
Discretionary Recognition	• Used to reward an individual, team or department for their significant contributions above and aside from the incentive recognition program	• Instrumental in saving a major account • Initiated an operational change that saved the organization $5K per month
Soft Recognition	• Reinforce behaviors that you want repeated • Catching an employee in the act of doing things right	• Letting an employee know how much you appreciated a specific instance where they went above and beyond the call of duty

It is important to consider the pros and cons for the different forms of recognition:

Form of recognition	+	-
Incentive	<ul><li>People know up front what it takes to be recognized</li><li>It supports achievement of the desired results</li><li>It sends a message that employee contributions are valued</li></ul>	<ul><li>If achievement is out of reach, people may perceive it as disingenuous</li><li>If achievement is set too low and is regularly achieved, it can be costly</li></ul>
Discretionary	<ul><li>People are being recognized</li></ul>	<ul><li>If applied inconsistently it can be a de-motivator</li><li>There can be perceived inequity</li><li>Can be viewed as a lack of commitment to recognition as a whole</li><li>Recognition doesn't happen</li></ul>
Soft Recognition	<ul><li>People feel appreciated</li><li>They know their manager noticed their contributions</li><li>It is the least expensive form of recognition</li><li>It is easy to deliver</li><li>It can be used cross-functionally</li></ul>	<ul><li>Inconsistent application</li><li>Perceived favoritism</li><li>Important contributions may be missed</li><li>Recognition doesn't happen</li></ul>

My recommendation is that you develop a formal recognition plan using incentive recognition as the basis. Then agree on whether discretionary recognition will be used and what boundaries need to be followed when using it. If more emphasis needs to be placed on informal recognition, a healthy discussion, agreements, and boundaries will be useful as you communicate and implement your new recognition plan.

Incentive recognition examples:

The following format can be used to build a comprehensive recognition plan for your team or organization.

Achievement	Frequency	Who Is Eligible	Award	How Awarded
115% of sales plan	Quarterly	All Sales Reps	$100.00	Quarterly Sales Meeting
0 Customer complaints	Monthly	Customer Service Team	Team Lunch	1st Team meeting monthly

Congratulations! With clear direction, team, department, and individual expectations aligned with direction, and with a performance management process in place, people being held accountable for delivering performance, and your people being recognized for their contributions...

You and your team or organization should be delivering consistent, sustainable performance!

Getting Results
Insights: **Tips:**

Insights:	Tips:
• Metrics are essential to delivering consistently strong performance. • Metrics serve as the basis for gauging progress and success. • If you never allow a performance hole to be dug, there will be no need to have to dig out of it. • Done right, recognition motivates employees. • Done wrong, recognition can be a de-motivator. • Reward and recognition should be designed to support performance achievement and reinforce needed behaviors.	• Use performance trends to stay on top of performance. • Inspect what you expect. • Intervene early to get things back on course. • Consider the planned level of performance the minimum acceptable level of performance. • Strive to exceed the planned level of performance. • Hold people accountable for delivering the desired levels of performance.

For information about available products and services visit www.businesspaths.net

What challenges are you facing?

Do you need to do more with less?
Improve performance?
Reduce turnover?

Contact *businessPATHS* to help you:

√ Pinpoint priorities
√ Set clear direction
√ Get people engaged
√ Improve how things are done

√ Develop your people
√ Create and develop teams
√ Build in accountability
√ Deliver consistent results

Are you planning a retreat?
Searching for a guest speaker?
Someone to conduct workshops?
Trying to find a facilitator?

---

businessPATHS Services:

Strategic Planning
Tactical Planning
Leadership development
Seminars

Executive coaching
Leadership coaching
Team development
Workshops

Contact *businessPATHS*…your partner in success…at www.businesspaths.net
or power10@businesspaths.net

Suggested Reading

Becoming a High Performance Manager, Harvard Business School Press

Includes a compilation of articles that allow managers to check their behaviors against recommended in a variety of areas such as time management, delegation and accountability.

Execution: The Discipline of Getting Things Done, Larry Bassidy, Ram Charan and Charles Burck

Provides insights into how effective execution, which poses a challenge for many organizations, supports and positively impacts the achievement of results.

Fierce Conversations: Achieving Success at Work and in Life, One Conversation at a Time, Susan Scott

Helps managers get honest with themselves, build empowerment and communicate what decisions should be made by others. It includes simple approaches to difficult situations and introduces tools to help people connect deeply with others.

Good to Great: Why Some Companies Make the Leap...and Others Don't, Jim Collins

Addresses the practices that move good, mediocre and even bad companies to solid, outstanding performance and enduring greatness.

Leading Change, John P. Kotter

Is a visionary yet practical guide to help managers lead in the 21st century. It includes an eight step process for creating major change and reveals the most common errors that inhibit successful change.

On Becoming a Leader, Warren Bennis

Is an excellent study in leadership and points out the differences between managing and leading. It includes the qualities of effective leaders, allowing managers to confirm what they do well, learn new leadership skills and develop into the best leader he or she can be.

The Carrot Principle: How the Best Managers Use Recognition to Engage Their People, Retain Talent, and Accelerate Performance, Adrian Gostick and Chester Elton

Reveals the importance and impact of recognition on productivity, engagement and retention. It includes results from one of the most in-depth management studies on the impact of recognition, and includes 125 recognition ideas.

The Orange Revolution: How One Great Team Can Transform and Entire Organization, Adrien Gostick and Chester Elton

Is a ground-breaking guide to building high-performance teams. It reveals how break-through teams operate and how managers can transform his or her team into a high performing team.

The Speed of Trust: The One Thing That Changes Everything, Stephen M.R. Covey and Rebecca R. Merrill

Addresses the importance and impact of trust in relationships, teams and organizations. It gets to the core of ethical behavior and integrity and how 'trust' is the most critical factor in effective leaders and organizations.

Zapp! The Lightening of Empowerment: How to Improve Quality, Productivity, and Employee Satisfaction, William C. Byham and Jeff Cox

A fable about empowering people to improve how the work is done and performance is achieved. It shares how managers can create a situation where employees take ownership for their jobs and improve the performance of their team and organization.

Glossary

20/50/30 rule—A rule of thumb dealing with resistance to change; 20 percent are for it, 50 percent are on the fence, and 30 percent are resistant to the change

20/80 rule—A rule of thumb relating to effort and result; i.e., 20 percent of customers generate 80 percent of the sales

Barriers—Hurdles or obstacles to accomplishing something

Benchmark—Something that serves as a standard by which others may be measured or judged

Bottom-line—Concerned only with cost or profits

Boundaries—Guidelines that indicate or establish a limit or extent

Brainstorming—A group problem-solving technique that involves the spontaneous contribution of ideas from all members of the group

Centralized decision-making—Decisions made by a select group of individuals

Change agent—A person who leads change efforts

Coaching—Instructing, directing, or prompting someone to do better

Collaboration—Working jointly with others or together to accomplish something

Command and control—A management approach where people are told what to do and how to do it

Competency—Having the knowledge and skills to perform specific roles effectively

Competitive advantage—Something that positions an organization ahead of its competition

Consensus—General agreement that everyone can support because it was reached in a fair and equitable manner

Continuous improvement—An ongoing focus and process, where people find new and more effective ways to run the day-to-day business and deliver results

Contributing factor—Something that influences or contributes to a condition or outcome

Coxswain—The on-the-water coach of the rowing crew

Critical few—A handful of top priorities

Cross-functional—Involving all functions in an organization

Customer value—Specifics about a product, service, or organization that drive the customer purchase decision

Decision authority—Having both responsibility and accountability for given decisions

Delegate—to appoint as one's representative

Desired state—Where a given situation or condition needs to be

Direct control—Where individuals or groups have full responsibility and authority over given situations

Discretionary recognition—Used to reward an individual, team, or department for their significant contributions above and aside from the incentive recognition program

***Doing* activities**—Activities managers perform that are the responsibility of others

Drill-down—Look below the surface to understand contributing factors and conditions

Employer of choice—An organization that has built a work environment and culture that attracts and retains more quality employees than it needs

Empowerment—Where managers and leaders give employees the responsibility and decision-authority to handle various areas of the organization

Entitlement—Employees believe they are deserving of certain privileges

External customer—Those who purchase an organization's products or services

Front-line managers—Those managers closest to the customer

Future state—The condition or situation an organization or team strives to achieve

Gap Analysis—A method for determining the difference between where a condition or situation is today and where it needs to be in the future

Goals and objectives—The end toward which effort is directed

Honest broker—A neutral mediator

Incentive recognition—Pre-determined levels of performance that must be met to receive recognition

Informal feedback—Sharing insights and recommendations on situations as you observe them

Innovation—The introduction of something new; a new idea, method, or device

Internal customer—Those people in the organization that benefit from your leadership

Intervene—to interfere with the outcome or course especially of a condition or process

Key focus area—A part of the business that is considered a priority

Lagging indicators—Metrics that reflect the final outcome or result of actions

Leading indicators—Metrics that allow you to gauge progress toward achievement of a goal

Lean Manufacturing—A production practice focused on increasing efficiency, decreasing waste, and using empirical methods to decide what matters, rather than uncritically accepting pre-existing ideas

Management Information—A set of metrics compiled to display ongoing and summary performance

Measures—A system of standard units to gauge progress and success

Metrics—Standards of measurement used to gauge progress and success

Mission—Defines the unique purpose, or the fundamental reason, for the organization's existence

Norming—The third stage of team development

One-way communication—Communication that flows in only one direction

Open-ended questions—Questions that require more than a yes or no answer

Organizational flattening—The process of reducing the number of layers between the President/CEO and the customer

Outcomes—A result of consequences of something

Output—Something produced by an individual or group

Partnerships—People joined together working toward a mutually successful outcome

Performing—The fourth stage of team development

power10—A rowing term that directs the crew to deliver ten of their best, perfectly timed, most powerful strokes to pull ahead of a competitor in the race

Practical solutions—Methods that can be used to address problems or seize opportunities

Primary customer—External or internal customers that are your top priority

Principles—Comprehensive and fundamental laws, doctrines, or assumptions

Results—The outcome from a consequence, effect, or conclusion

Re-work—The need to redo something that wasn't done right the first time

Root cause—The underlying reason for a given condition

S.M.A.R.T. Test—A method used to ensure that goals and objectives are specific, measurable, attainable, relevant, and time-based

Say the words—Share open, honest feedback

Self-directed team—A group of people working together to run their day-to-day business with minimal management involvement

Servant Leadership—Leaders giving priority attention to the needs of their colleagues and those they serve to achieve results for the organization

Situational Leadership—Leaders need to adapt to a given situation by choosing the appropriate directing, coaching, supporting, or delegating approach.

Six Sigma—A strategy for improving the quality of process outputs by identifying and removing the causes of defects and minimizing variability in manufacturing and business processes

Soft recognition—Thanking people for doing a great job or going the extra mile while finding them in the act of doing something right

Standard operating procedures—Established or prescribed methods to be followed routinely for the performance of designated operations or in designated situations

Status quo—The existing state of affairs

Status reviews—Sessions where people with assigned responsibilities report on progress and success

Storming—The second stage of team development

Strategic initiatives—Over-arching priorities for the organization

Stretch goals—Goals that will take extra effort to achieve

Success factors—Key things that influence and contribute to a successful outcome

Task force—A temporary grouping under one leader for the purpose of accomplishing a definite objective

Top-down communication—Set messages initiated at the executive levels that roll out through the organization

Transactional Leadership—Leaders give clear instructions about what their expectations are. When those expectations are fulfilled, there are rewards, and failure is severely punished. Work is allocated to subordinates whether resources are there or absent.

Transformational Leadership—Focuses on "transforming" others to help each other, to look out for each other, to be encouraging and harmonious, and to look out for the organization as a whole. The leader enhances the motivation, morale, and performance of his or her follower group.

Two-way communication—An exchange where parties share thoughts and ideas with each other

Up-time—The percentage of time that equipment is running at standard

Value-added work—Performing those activities that provide the greatest payback to customers

Values—Describe how an organization wants people to act, consistent with attainment of the Vision and Mission

Vision—A compelling picture of the future that describes what the organization is striving to achieve. It inspires people to rally behind the effort and willingly take part in the journey.

Webinars—A host-led presentation that participants access from their computer

What's* and *how's—Strategy and tactics respectively

Win-win—A situation where parties reach mutually beneficial agreements and outcomes

Work process—Steps employees follow to consistently perform given tasks

INDEX

www.ingramcontent.com/pod-product-compliance
Lightning Source LLC
Chambersburg PA
CBHW081116170526
45165CB00008B/2464